Getting Ready for the Wedding

Resources by Les and Leslie Parrott

Books

Becoming Soul Mates
Getting Ready for the Wedding
Love Is
The Marriage Mentor Manual
Meditations on Proverbs for Couples
Questions Couples Ask
Relationships
Relationships Workbook
Saving Your Marriage Before It Starts
Saving Your Marriage Before It Starts Workbook for Men
Saving Your Marriage Before It Starts Workbook for Women
Saving Your Second Marriage Before It Starts
Saving Your Second Marriage Before It Starts Workbook for Men
Saving Your Second Marriage Before It Starts Workbook for Women

Video Curriculum—Zondervan*Groupware*™

Relationships
Saving Your Marriage Before It Starts
Mentoring Engaged and Newlywed Couples

Audio Pages®

Relationships
Saving Your Marriage Before It Starts
Saving Your Second Marriage Before It Starts

Books by Les Parrott III

High Maintenance Relationships
Seven Secrets of a Healthy Dating Relationship

Getting Ready for the Wedding

All You Need to Know Before
You Say I Do

Les & Leslie Parrott
General Editors

ZONDERVAN™

GRAND RAPIDS, MICHIGAN 49530

ZONDERVAN™

Getting Ready for the Wedding
Copyright © 1998 by Les and Leslie Parrott

Requests for information should be addressed to:

Zondervan, *Grand Rapids, Michigan 49530*

Library of Congress Cataloging-in-Publication Data

Parrott, Les.
   Getting ready for the wedding : all you need to know before you say I do
/ Les and Leslie Parrott.
      p.   cm.
      ISBN: 0-310-21148-4 (pbk.)
      1. Marriage. 2. Marriage—Religious aspects—Christianity. 3. Betrothal.
4. Weddings. I. Parrott, Leslie L., 1964– . II. Title.
HQ734.P213 1997
306.81-dc 21   97-30560

Interior design by Sue Vandenberg Koppenol

Printed in the United States of America

01 02 03 04 05 06 /❖ DC/ 12 11 10 9 8 7 6

Contents

Preface

Leslie and I had just completed a series of marriage seminars in Singapore and were waiting in the Tokyo airport while in transit. Exhausted and groggy, I was forcing myself to stay interested in the book I was trying to read when I looked up to notice a person sitting across from me.

"I know that guy. Who is he?" I whispered to Leslie. "I *know* I know him."

"We're going to be here for the next four hours," she replied. "Why don't you ask him?"

"Nah, it'll come to me."

An hour later, it did. It was Robert McNamara, Secretary of Defense who worked in the Johnson, Kennedy, and Nixon administrations—the one man, more responsible than any other, for getting the United States involved in the Vietnam War. I felt compelled to talk with him.

"I don't mean to trouble you . . . ," I started in. We talked for the next half hour. It turned out that he was on a tour through Asia promoting his controversial book, *In Retrospect*, in which he confesses to the mistake of getting our country into a war we could never win. In the context of our conversation I asked this seventy-something man why he wrote such a self-incriminating book. He didn't hesitate for a moment. "I wanted this generation to learn from my mistakes," he said.

In a sense, the book you hold in your hands was written for the very same reason. When it comes to getting ready for a wedding and preparing for marriage, much can be learned from those who have gone before you. With their advantages of experience and perspective, they can show you how to avoid the mistakes others have made and help make your engagement, wedding, and marriage everything they were meant to be.

Whether you are just a few weeks away from your wedding day or standing on the brink of engagement, this book is for you.

It brings together a variety of specialists who openly and honestly talk about ten critical issues for making the days that lead up to your wedding (and all the years that follow) an overwhelming success. We've worked with hundreds of engaged couples, and, since the release of our book *Saving Your Marriage Before It Starts*, we've learned that many miss out on what should be a wonderful time of celebration and anticipation because they became more engaged to a wedding than they did to each other. We've also learned that with a little bit of practical advice, these same couples could make their engagements a meaningful time of laying the foundation for lasting love.

So, with this in mind, we asked some of the most insightful and experienced experts to guide you through your engagement.

What to Expect from This Book

In this book, you won't find advice on selecting the color of your bridesmaids' dresses, choosing a caterer, or selecting wedding stationery. We'll leave that to the bridal magazines and wedding consultants. What we won't leave to them, however, are the more important issues that go into having a meaningful and successful engagement—the heartfelt issues that can make or break this important period in your life.

No book has ever really addressed the things that matter most for having a great engagement, but we are pleased to bring you, chapter by chapter, some of the wisest counsel you will ever find on the topic.

We begin in chapter 1 with the most fundamental question engaged couples ask: How do I know if I'm really ready for marriage? Here you will learn the most common reasons for getting married and assess your own motivations for matrimony. This chapter will bolster your confidence and lay a foundation for the chapters that follow.

Dave and Claudia Arp, in chapter 2, show you the ins and outs of how to have a great engagement. It's not as easy as you might think, but they reveal some proven strategies for taking much of the stress out of your months of engagement.

Chapter 3 gets down to brass tacks by exploring how to get married without drowning in debt. Whether you are paying for your wedding yourself or working within somebody else's budget, financial expert Ron Blue provides a proven strategy for keeping your wedding bills from drowning out your wedding bells.

It's not at all uncommon for one or both of you to experience wedding jitters as the big day approaches. In fact, they're normal. Robert and Rosemary Barnes, in chapter 4, give you a step-by-step plan for helping these jitters work for you rather than against you.

So much planning goes into the wedding day that many couples forget to enjoy it. Without the guidance of Dave and Jan Stoop's expert advice in chapter 5, the "happiest day of your life" is in jeopardy of being one of the most stressful and pressure packed.

In chapter 6, Cliff and Joyce Penner provide a frank and honest discussion of what you need to know to have a great wedding night and a wonderful honeymoon. Whatever your sexual history, you will find this chapter brimming with wise and practical advice for getting your sex life off to a great start.

On many occasions a couple deeply in love has asked us the painful question: What do we do when our parents don't approve? We now have an answer. Actually John Trent has an answer in chapter 7. With great care and sensitivity, he provides the tools you'll need for resolving this situation and making a healthy decision together.

After all the hype and planning that goes into a wedding celebration, you may not be surprised by the almost inevitable post-party letdown. But many couples experience "wedding-bell blues." In chapter 8, Norm Wright will help you recover from this common malady if and when it strikes, and help prepare you for a great first year of marriage.

Perhaps you are reading this book because you are getting married for the second time and want to do it right. We commend you. And Tom Whiteman knows firsthand that you have unique concerns. In chapter 9 he addresses these issues head-on and shows you how to resolve past pain and renew your spirit for your upcoming wedding.

After the rice is thrown, the rented tuxedos returned, the honeymoon trip completed, and the last thank-you note written, you'll begin to set up house together. And as you unpack your belongings and put away your new dishes, we want to make sure your marriage—not just your wedding and honeymoon—is a success. So we dedicate chapter 10 to getting your marriage started on the right foot with some practical exercises and creative suggestions that will help you do just that.

With every good wish and prayer,

Les and Leslie Parrott
Center for Relationship Development
Seattle Pacific University

How to Know When You're Ready for Marriage

Les and Leslie Parrott

I wish I had a photographer at my first "wedding." I was deliriously happy even though it happened so quickly. I don't remember much about the groom, Devon Newkirk, but I was a picture-book bride. I wore one of my mother's silky half-slips draped over my head like a veil and was dressed all in white—except for my black tennis shoes. Devon and I were six years old, and the setting was my backyard. The ceremony was followed by a beautiful reception with graham crackers slathered in white frosting.

We pin our hopes for happiness on romantic love so early in life. In elementary school, before my faux nuptials in the backyard, I desperately wanted to marry Chris, a fellow kindergartner. Later, when I was twelve and the *Brady Bunch* was a hit TV show, I believed with all my heart that if Greg Brady ever laid eyes on me, I would be his forever.

The longing for a profound, all-consuming connection with a marriage partner is in our very wiring. The yearning for fulfillment through love seems to be to our psychic structure what food and water are to our cells.

Consider the stories that have shaped our consciousness: Beauty and the Beast, Snow White and her handsome prince, Cinderella and Prince Charming. It's not just these lucky fairy-tale characters of childhood who have captured our collective imagination, however. We're constantly bombarded by visions of romance. All you have to do is turn on the radio or television or open any magazine. Everywhere we turn, we're faced with glamorized versions of love.

Trying to forge an authentic relationship amidst all the romantic hype makes what is already a tough proposition even harder. It leaves many wondering whether they are falling in love with a person or simply with love itself. And once the proverbial question is popped and the wedding machine is set in motion, it leaves many wondering whether they are really ready to get hitched in the first place.

Whether you are knee-deep in doubt or just wanting to bolster your relational confidence, this chapter will help you clear your head, wipe the stars from your eyes, and cut through the glamour and glitz to determine your "marital readiness quotient." We begin by exploring ten reasons people *shouldn't* get married, then highlight the one reason for marriage that matters most. The rest of the chapter is devoted to a self-test for measuring your marital readiness—both personally and relationally.

Ten Reasons People Shouldn't Get Married

Ask most engaged couples why they are getting married and the answer is automatic: "Because we are in love." But if you scratch the surface you'll find that the motivations for matrimony are far more complex. A combination of many complicated situations and needs motivate most people to marry, some reasons being better than others. In fact, some reasons for marrying improve your chances of success, while others work against it. What follows, briefly, are ten terrible reasons for marriage—reasons that researchers term "deficits."

1. Love at first sight seems like a romantic reason for marriage, but it's not a good predictor of marital success. Not that strong feelings of attraction cannot occur early in a relationship. They can. But such feelings alone provide a weak foundation for a long-lasting relationship. Just watch the dozens of Hollywood marriages each year that are ignited on a studio lot and break up after only a year or two of wedded disaster.

2. Rebounding also hinders the chances for marital longevity. It's a proven fact that people fall in love more easily when they're on the rebound. Research has found that people suffer low self-esteem after a breakup and are far less discriminating in choosing a partner because they are trying to cope with their loss.[1] To marry on the rebound is undesirable because the wedding occurs as a reaction to a previous partner, rather than being based on real love for the new partner.

3. Rebellion leads some into a marital mismatch. Getting even with parents, for example, by marrying someone they do not like is not uncommon, but it's always costly. The truth is, parental interference can increase feelings of romantic attraction between partners—social-psychologists call it the "Romeo and Juliet effect."[2] As with marriage on the rebound, the wedding is a response to someone else (one's parents) rather than to one's partner.

4. Loneliness can sometimes drive a person into a hasty marriage. This is especially true among the divorced and widowed.[3] The problem with this motivation is that lonely people will end up lonely in marriage if the relationship doesn't have much more of a foundation to stand on. In other words, it is the relationship rather than the institution that banishes loneliness.

5. Obligation sometimes substitutes for love when considering marriage. Some partners marry because one of them feels too guilty to break it off. A woman who marries a man because she believes her loyal devotion and encouragement will help him quit drinking and live up to his potential could be an example of this. Such marriages often don't work. The helper finds that his or her partner won't change so easily, and the pitied partner comes to resent being the object of a crusade.

6. *Financial advancement* is a marriage motivator for some. Many young divorced mothers consider remarriage primarily because they are exhausted from the struggle of supporting and caring for their small children.[4] Men, too, can marry to advance their career in some professions. The person going into marriage mainly for economic reasons, however, is not a likely candidate for marrying well.

7. *Sexual attraction* and guilt over sexual involvement are popular but weak reasons for marriage. Sex is not a sufficient reason to marry and seldom leads to lifelong happiness. In fact, the sexual chemistry between two people often blinds the partners to other important relational qualities.

8. *Premarital pregnancy* is a growing problematic reason for marriage, and a great deal of recent research has identified a consistent relationship between it and divorce. Ironically, teenage women who marry to avoid single parenthood often become single parents after all. There are several reasons for this. First, the marriage is forced by outside events instead of internal desire and commitment. Second, babies are expensive, and financial stress on a marriage is always difficult. Finally, the couple may not even be compatible enough for marriage and may end up resenting each other.[5] It is difficult to be encouraging about young, pregnancy-inspired marriages, and some churches have been reluctant to sanction them unless the young couple is unusually mature.

9. *Escape* is perhaps the most damaging motivation for marriage. Some people marry to escape an unhappy home situation, but hoping that a new person or a new environment will be better is a terrible basis for marriage. Usually the person who marries to escape will go through a series of relational failures. This person will eventually "escape" one marriage for another and then another. Such people believe that a new relationship

could not be worse than their present one and are almost always surprised to find out that it is.

10. Pressure from parents, peers, and society in general pushes some singles into marriage. Research shows that this can be particularly true for women, but for either gender, the expectations built up during courtship exert a great deal of social pressure to go through with the marriage.[6] The more one is identified as a couple, the more difficult it is to back out of an engagement. You should know, however, that breaking an engagement is less stressful than divorcing later or being unhappily married. By the way, about 100,000 couples decide to break their engagements each year.[7]

The Marriage Motivation Test

On a scale of 1 to 10, rate how much of a factor each of the following motivators are for you to get married. Take time to consider each item, and be as honest as possible.

1. Love at first sight is a significant factor in why I'm ready to get married.

Not at All True   *Extremely True of Me*
1   2   3   4   5   6   7   8   9   10

2. Rebounding from the pain of a previous relationship is a significant factor in my motivation for marriage.

Not at All True   *Extremely True of Me*
1   2   3   4   5   6   7   8   9   10

3. Rebellion against my parent's disapproval is a primary factor in my motivation.

Not at All True   *Extremely True of Me*
1   2   3   4   5   6   7   8   9   10

4. Loneliness contributes significantly to my reasons for getting married.

Not at All True   *Extremely True of Me*
1   2   3   4   5   6   7   8   9   10

5. A sense of obligation and even pity and guilt are significant factors in motivating me to marry.

Not at All True   *Extremely True of Me*
1   2   3   4   5   6   7   8   9   10

6. Financial advancement weighs heavily on my decision to get married.

Not at All True   *Extremely True of Me*
1   2   3   4   5   6   7   8   9   10

7. Sexual attraction is the most important factor driving me to get married at this time.

Not at All True   *Extremely True of Me*
1   2   3   4   5   6   7   8   9   10

8. Premarital pregnancy is the primary reason pushing me into marriage.

Not at All True   *Extremely True of Me*
1   2   3   4   5   6   7   8   9   10

9. Escape from an unhappy home life is causing me to want to get married.

Not at All True   *Extremely True of Me*
1   2   3   4   5   6   7   8   9   10

10. Pressure from parents, peers, or society has a lot to do with why I am getting married.

Not at All True   *Extremely True of Me*
1   2   3   4   5   6   7   8   9   10

Scoring: Add up your score from each of the ten items. There are 100 possible points on this test. If your score is 15 or less you can rest easy in the fact that you are probably not getting married for some of the most common negative reasons. If your score is greater than 15 you will certainly want to do some soul-searching on your own and with your partner about the items that you ranked highest. We also strongly suggest that you discuss these motivators with an objective counselor.

The Most Important Marriage Motivator

We have seen that rebounding, rebellion, escape, loneliness, obligation, sex, pressure, and all the rest are not likely predictors of a happy marriage. In fact, if you are primarily motivated by any one of them, you should pause to think about your engagement. Postponing a marriage date, for example, may give you the time you need to consider why you are marrying in the first place. By the way, it's not wrong to break off an engagement to reconsider your motivations. About one in four engaged couples break up temporarily for that very reason.[8] We did.

After six-and-a-half years of dating and nearly five months of being engaged, I (Leslie) was having second thoughts. Can you believe it? When Les proposed to me I said yes without thinking about it. Literally. We had dated so long that I took our relationship, as well as our eventual marriage, for granted. We never shopped together for wedding rings, and the night in Chicago that Les surprised me with his proposal was terribly romantic. I said yes out of instinct.

> *To love
> and be loved
> by another person
> is perhaps
> the single
> most satisfying
> experience on earth.*

After our engagement was official, however, I began feeling as though I hadn't really decided on marriage for myself. It felt more like it was Les's decision and his timing, not ours, that was taking us to the chapel. My doubts were strong enough for me to break it off, at least temporarily, and see a counselor. A month or two later the decision to get married was as much mine as it was his. That was in 1984, and since then neither of us has ever doubted for one second the decision to marry each other.

Part of the reason for our marital success may be that we married, not out of a deficit, but out of a motivation that researchers say is the most important: *companionship*.[9] To love and be loved by another person is perhaps the single most satisfying experience on earth. Many of the benefits of companionship can be enjoyed without marriage, of course, but marriage provides the social structure for experiencing this phenomenon most deeply. Marriage provides a configuration, a form, an institution for two souls to walk together through life. It provides a covenant whereby soul mates pledge to love each other in good times and bad, in sickness and in health—to have and to hold as companions unto death.

Our prayer is that you and your partner are getting married for all the right reasons, that your marital motivations are pure. If that's the case, it's now time to turn your attention to your marital readiness.

Marks of Marital Readiness

Preparing for the wedding has been compared to readying for a trip into the wild unknown. The wedding dress and bride's trousseau, according to some, need to be as carefully set as a compass pointed toward new territory. As Dr. Mary Roberts wrote in her 1912 book *Why Women Are So*, "A trousseau was as essential to the prospective bride as an outfit to the explorer of arctic or tropical wilds . . . who knows what might be needed and yet unattainable in the great adventure upon which she was about to embark!"

To prepare the trousseau, a prospective bride spent her engagement stitching linens and clothing. She sewed and shopped, packed and cleaned, sewed and packed some more. The process became her transition into wifehood, and she certainly wanted to come out of it looking her absolute best.

A century later, some of us may think that we modern women have moved beyond that. Clearly, we've become more cultured through our careers and our educations. But the wedding dress is still a big deal. Big enough to create a stampede at the Filene's bargain basement wedding dress sale. You may have heard of this rough-and-tumble ritual that happens each year beneath the streets of Boston.

Wedding plans seem far more tangible than marriage.

On the single day of the sale, hundreds of prospective brides from around the country descend on the department store. Within sixty seconds of the store's opening, they have scavenged all eight hundred dresses off the racks. Without a modicum of modesty, the brides-to-be strip to their underwear in the middle of the store, tug on white gowns, and elbow in at the mirrors. Zippers get stripped, hems get soiled, lace gets torn. But the dresses at Filene's that day are so cheap that no one cares about the later cost of alterations and cleaning. The object is simply to find the dress of one's dreams and get one step closer to being ready for the wedding.

Overlooked in the excitement of planning a wedding, however, is the fact that being prepared for the wedding does not equal being prepared for marriage. You may have a beautiful diamond ring and the wedding dress of your dreams. You may be holding two airline tickets to a romantic honeymoon getaway while your pressed tuxedo hangs neatly in your closet. You may have sent out calligraphy invitations to one hundred of your closest friends. You may have your wedding planned down to the finest little detail, but the truth remains: *Being prepared for your wedding does not equal being prepared for your marriage.*

It's understandable that some couples spend more time preparing for their weddings than they do for their marriage. Wedding plans seem far more tangible. Once the caterer is scheduled, you can check it off your to-do list. Relational readiness is not so tidy. In recent years, however, experts have made great strides in identifying the qualities that reveal whether or not a couple is really ready for marriage. You can think of their findings as a kind of checklist—a checklist divided into two parts: personal readiness and relational readiness.

Personal Readiness

Walk into the office of any marriage expert and ask what personal qualities are most important for the soon-to-be spouse, and you may get an earful. The list, to say the least, would be long. But if we were to boil all of the responses down to a minimum, you would probably end up with at least these three: a healthy self-concept, personal maturity, and independence from your family of origin.

Self-concept refers to your mental and emotional well-being, and it's built on two qualities: knowing who you are and liking who you are. A mountain of research shows that a fragile self-concept leaves one susceptible to a marital mismatch (as well as personal problems such as depression), while a healthy self-concept (for both you and your partner) is predictive of a fully functioning marriage—one that will not only go the distance but be extremely fulfilling. When conflict arises, for example, two people with a healthy self-concept have the internal resources required to work it out. Those with a poor self-concept are prone to deny the conflict exists or react defensively to any suggestion of compromise. They don't have the emotional reserves to navigate the inevitable tough times, and the marriage pays the price.

Psychologist Dr. Neil Warren has written extensively about this fact in his wonderful book *Finding the Love of Your Life*. One night over dinner, we asked Neil why he gives so much attention to a person's self-concept before they get married. He didn't hesitate for a minute: "A marriage can only be as healthy as the least healthy person in that partnership." How true. In a very real sense, a lack of emotional well-being is hazardous to your marriage. So we echo the sentiments of our friend Neil: Get healthy before you get married.

Maturity, if we are honest, comes with age. And social scientists have found that one's age says a lot about your readiness for marriage. Did you know that people in their twenties or older are far more likely to have successful marriages than those who marry in their teens? In fact, marriages among teenagers are twice as likely to end in divorce as marriages of those in their twenties. Even more astounding, the divorce rate for twenty-one- and twenty-two-year-olds is twice as high as it is for twenty-four and twenty-five-year-olds. After the age of thirty, the divorce rate remains more consistent.

Age itself is probably not the key variable in determining the likelihood of a marriage succeeding. Rather, it seems likely that age is simply correlated with preparedness and wisdom. Age is correlated with maturity or ripeness—the state of being ready. We've known many young people who are quite mature, and we've known plenty of older people who are not. But generally speaking, with age comes maturity. And the more mature, the more prepared one is for marriage. It's no mistake that maturity and matrimony come from the same Latin origin.

Independence is all about your relationship with your family of origin, or more specifically, your mother and father. Your relationship with your parents shapes your ability to relate with others—including your fiancé—more than you might think. At conscious and unconscious levels, they taught you to either trust people or fear them, to be intimate or stay distant, to express your feelings or keep them private.

Much of your personal readiness for marriage depends on the state of your relationship with your parents. What lessons from home will you bring into your marriage? Is there unresolved pain in relation to your parents that you still need to work through? "A child who has painful experiences early in life," writes marriage expert Harville Hendrix, "will either feel cut off from those around him or will attempt to fuse with them [and become] a recurring problem in marriage."[10] Before entering marriage, you need to carefully examine your parental relationships to ensure that your partner becomes your most important relational priority.

We counseled a newly married couple who lives more than a thousand miles away from the bride's parents, but she will barely make a move before phoning home to get Dad's advice. Whether it be about how to arrange the furniture or what to have for dinner, she wants his input. Needless to say, her new husband began wondering whether he was even necessary. Similarly, another couple we worked with was struggling because the groom consulted his father on financial decisions without including his new wife. In this case, with little or no say in how their money was invested, she felt discounted and ignored. These are typical scenarios for men and women who don't achieve a healthy individual identity and sense of independence before getting married.

We hope you have a close and connected relationship with your parents. And, if so, we hope you will work hard to maintain it. But for your marriage to work, you must make sure you are in a place to have your partner, not your parents, be your top priority.

Relational Readiness

Assessing the personal qualities of self-concept, maturity, and independence is only half of the journey toward determining your marital readiness. The second half has to do, not with personal qualities, but with the relational qualities you share with your partner. Once again we whittle away at a long list to examine the bare essentials. If you and your partner are ready for marriage, your relationship will be characterized by longevity, stability, and similarity.

Longevity has to do with how long you have known each other and dated. We work on a university campus and have discovered a disturbing syndrome afflicting a good portion of every senior class. It's called the "ring-by-spring" syndrome. That's the humorous way of putting it. But when two people decide to jump into marriage too quickly, it's no laughing matter.

Research on mate selection makes it clear: Couples who rush into matrimony are at significant risk. Neil Warren points to a study conducted at Kansas State University in which "a strong correlation was found between length of time spent dating" and "marital satisfaction." The researchers discovered that "couples who had dated for more than two years scored consistently high on marital satisfaction, while couples who had dated for shorter periods scored in a wide range from very high to very low."[11] The point is that the longer you date, the more ready you are for marriage.

If you have been dating for less than two years, it doesn't mean you are predestined to dissatisfaction in marriage. It just means that the risk of that happening is higher. So why take the risk? In our relational readiness assessment, we strongly recommend that you not leap into marriage if you have only known each other less than a year at the very minimum. We understand that the time you have been together may be the most romantic months you could ever dream of, but there is no need to rush. Give yourselves time and increase your chances of sharing a married love that will go the distance. After all, marriage is for the rest of your lives, and if you think you are ready for that kind of commitment after only a few short months, you better think again. Our ideal is at least two years from the first date to the wedding day.

Stability is the quality of having constancy, reliability, dependability, and steadfastness. If these terms characterize your relationship, that's a good sign. Far too many unsteady couples wobble their way to the altar—as if just getting there was the point. It's not. The point is to get there in a stable and steadfast condition. Why? Once again, this quality increases the probability of fulfillment in marriage. Couples whose courtships are characterized by conflict, turbulence, and those telltale on-again/off-again starts and stops—in a word, instability—are far less likely to find happiness in marriage.

Stability in the dating years indicates that a couple is learning to practice negotiation and compromise. They are learning the fine art and skill of communication. In short, stable couples are proving to themselves in the dating years that they can navigate the turbulent and treacherous waters that are an inevitable part of sailing a marriage vessel. These couples are resolving conflicts and keeping an even keel. They are charting a steady course bound to bring them happiness.

As their dating journey brings them into a period of engagement, these stable couples are also practicing commitment. That commitment is part of their secret to stability. It's as if they are saying: "In spite of all the uncertainties of life, in spite of all the things I can't seem to nail down, I'm going to make one thing certain—my love for you and for our relationship." This kind of commitment comes from a cool head and a steadfast heart. And it's essential to assessing your relational readiness for marriage.

Similarity is not about feeling and doing everything exactly the same way. That's uniformity. Similarity is more like unity than uniformity. It has to do with holding common values, beliefs, and attitudes. Why is similarity important to your marriage? Because the happiest married couples have a lot in common. You may disagree, but it's a fact. Similarities—especially on the issues that matter most to each person—are the glue that holds them together. The more similarities two people share, the more likely their relationship will survive and thrive. It's that simple. After a careful review of many, many marital studies, researchers concluded that "similarity is associated with marital success and is less associated with marital instability and divorce."[12]

If a happy and committed couple has a lot in common, you may be wondering just what exactly these commonalities are. Role expectations for husband and wife certainly make the list. Do you and your partner view these the same way? Is your picture of what a wife should do or how a husband should behave similar? Values are another important issue. Do you share common values about spiritual matters, money, family, politics? Do you value them to the same degree and with the same passion? Other similarities to consider are desire for children, energy level, dependability, sense of hu-

Similarities are the glue that holds couples together.

mor, cleanliness, goals, interests, habits, skills.[13] The list is practically endless.

Well, does this emphasis on unity mean you shouldn't marry someone who is very different from you? Not necessarily. But if you do, you'd better have plenty of important similarities that outweigh and counteract your dissimilarities. Economic, racial, religious, political, intellectual, educational, and emotional similarities provide a common base of operation and make life significantly easier to negotiate together. Why? Because every difference requires time, energy, and work to find a middle ground, if there is one. The more differences between you, the more nooks and crannies you will discover in your relationship for resentment and frustration to hide. And the more stressful your marriage becomes.

So, as you consider your relational readiness for marriage, take time to examine your longevity, your stability, and your differences. The time you spend on this today may save you a lot of pain in the future.

The Marital Readiness Questionnaire

The following questions will help you assess your readiness for marriage. Be ruthlessly honest with yourself while answering these questions.

1. Do you know who you are and like who you are?
2. Would you say you generally have a healthy sense of self-esteem and confidence?
3. Do you feel comfortable talking about your differences in times of conflict (rather than ignoring them)?
4. Are you twenty years of age or older?
5. Are you twenty-four years of age or older?
6. Would people you respect say you are personally mature?
7. Would you say you have a good relationship with your mother and father?
8. Do you feel comfortable thinking for yourself and making your own decisions?
9. Are you able to make decisions without feeling compelled to please your parents?
10. Are you genuinely prepared to make your marriage relationship a higher priority than your relationship with your parents?
11. Have you resolved painful or troubling issues with your parents that may impact your marriage?
12. Have you identified specific quirks or qualities you may be bringing into your marriage as a result of growing up in your family of origin?
13. Have you dated your partner for a year or more?
14. Have you dated your partner for two years or more?
15. Are you willing to take your time in determining whether your relationship is ready for marriage?
16. Would you characterize your relationship as stable and steadfast?

17. Do you both practice effective compromise and negotiation in your relationship?
18. Can you both resolve conflict between you without losing control?
19. Are you 100 percent committed, beyond a shadow of a doubt, to making this relationship work?
20. Do you agree with all of your partner's important goals and values?
21. Do you and your partner share many similarities (e.g., sense of humor, habits, goals)?
22. Are your differences tiny compared to your similarities?
23. Do you and your partner have similar family backgrounds?
24. Do you rarely feel criticized or corrected by your partner?
25. Do you like this person as he/she is at this moment, without expecting him/her to change?

Scoring: Add up the number of yes responses from these items and multiply by four. That will give you a possible score of 100. If you answered honestly and your score is 90 or higher, your answers indicate you are probably ready for marriage. A score of 80 to 89 indicates that you are on your way, but you would probably be wise to give it more time and careful counsel. A score of 79 or lower indicates that you still have a great deal of work to do either personally or relationally before you are ready for marriage. You are likely to benefit from the help of a good counselor and more time. Whether your score is high or low, this brief assessment should serve simply as a guideline, not as the final answer.

One More Word

Whether or not you have avoided all of the wrong reasons people get married, and whether or not you are personally and relationally ready for marriage, we strongly recommend that you do whatever it takes to get some premarital training. As we said in *Saving Your Marriage Before It Starts*, the "till death do us part" of the marriage vow has become "till divorce do us part" for too many couples. But you don't have to be one of them. A little bit of premarriage work is like an immune shot against divorce for you and your partner.

Did you know that specialists can now predict with more than eighty percent accuracy—long before the wedding day—whether a marriage will succeed or fail? It's remarkable! Never has so much been known about what it takes to make marriage go the distance. And by meeting for just a few sessions with a trained minister or counselor (ask him or her about taking the PREPARE test), you will not only be ready for your wedding, but for the exhilarating and mysterious wonders of marriage.

2

Secrets of a Great Engagement

❧ David and Claudia Arp ❧

When we asked newlyweds how to have a great engagement, most laughed and replied, "Elope!"

While we knew this response was said tongue-in-cheek, we also knew that these couples were confessing how difficult engagements can sometimes be. After all, the whimsical lyrics, "Going to the chapel and we're going to get married," make it sound like engagements are a cakewalk. But they aren't. The months, weeks, and days that lead to your wedding can be wonderfully exciting as you plan your ceremony and reception, register for wedding gifts, schedule your honeymoon, and dream about your home together. But in all the excitement, new levels of stress—with your parents, future in-laws, friends, and even each other—are inevitable.

Some couples are so blinded by the stars in their eyes that they are certain they won't experience problems. If they do have

Don't get

so wrapped up

in planning

the future

that you forget

to enjoy

the present.

difficulties, they are sure their love will see them through anything. They are totally unprepared for the challenges that come with any engagement. But you can do some things now to insure that your engagement will be largely positive. We realize much of your time and energy in the next few months will be invested in planning for your wedding, but don't get so wrapped up in planning the future that you forget to enjoy the present. Find the balance that leads to a great engagement.

An engagement is about more than just the wedding. You wouldn't know it by checking out the plethora of brides' magazines at your local grocery store. You'll find everything you want to know about caterers, flowers, wedding attire, receptions, and even romantic honeymoon locations. But conspicuously missing is how to enjoy your relationship in the midst of your engagement.

A great engagement doesn't just happen—you *make* it happen by setting realistic goals and then working hard to achieve them. Actually, having a great engagement in those months before you get married could be compared to having a great pregnancy before you become parents. Both focus on the future and both are hard work—and usually not without some discomfort and suffering. And then the moment you've been waiting for, while thrilling, is over in a matter of hours. That's why it's important to focus now on ways you can make the most of the months leading up to your wedding day.

The rest of this chapter provides you with ten secrets of a great engagement. Following these guidelines will help you make the most of the months leading up to your wedding day. Not only that, but they will start you on the path toward a wonderfully lifelong marriage.

Choose to Stay Positive

Whatever challenges you face, choose to stay positive. Transitional times are stressful, but having a great engagement can lead to a great marriage. Now is your opportunity to develop a more positive outlook on life. This will have a ripple effect. Your attitude will affect your fiancé and others who are around you. So instead of seeing difficult situations as "problems," see them as avenues to growth.

We suggest you begin each morning with a simple prayer and Scripture reading. Spend time in Song of Songs or commit to memory 1 Corinthians 13, then reflect and give thanks. Your whole day will be brighter.

Spend time reminding yourself of your goal to enjoy this engagement process, minimize external stresses, and cherish your fiancé. Remind yourself of the strengths you bring to this partnership, and psyche yourself up to face the challenges of the day.

Put Closure on Your Life as a Single

During engagement you spend so much energy planning for the future that you may forget to say good-bye to the past. Have you considered what you will be giving up as a result of getting married? Are there activities and personal habits that will be forever altered because of your marriage? Perhaps you go out with your work friends every Friday evening. Or maybe you have a personal habit you know will have to change when your spouse moves in—you leave your dirty clothes lying on the bedroom floor, or you take up all the bathroom counter space with your cosmetics. Have you been living with your best friend from college for the last five years? Leaving that living situation may, in some ways, be as momentous as moving in with your new spouse. You'll need to grieve the loss of that familiarity and friendship as you celebrate finding your soul mate and cherished love in your spouse.

Your relationship with your parents will inevitably change as well. Separating from your home of origin will not only help you bring closure on your life as a single, but also will help you merge together as a couple. In the Genesis account of the first marriage, man was challenged to "leave" his father and mother and to "cleave" to his wife, becoming one flesh. Modern marriage emphasizes the "becoming one flesh," but just as important is breaking away from your family of origin and cleaving to each other.

While some aspects of singleness may be easily relinquished, others may be harder to give up. Of course you don't have to completely eliminate your other relationships or some of your solitary activities, but you will surely need to change many things about the way you now live. So instead of being surprised by how your life will change, identify the habits and activities you know need to end and bid them a fond farewell. You can make a creative ceremony out of your good-bye, develop a "twelve-step plan" for breaking a bad habit, or overindulge in the activity as a final blitz. But take charge of the process and put closure on your past now, when you have the time and the ability to say good-bye in your own way. After you are married you may be so consumed with building your new life that you may resent the sudden changes in habit you hadn't prepared for.

Marriage is like moving to a new city or town; your day-to-day living may be very different, but the excitement and challenges of a new circumstance will certainly be worth all that you give up. As you intentionally put closure on your life as a single, you will then be able to merge together and even subconsciously begin to think in terms of "we" instead of "me."

Merge Your Lives as You Plan for the Future

Merging your lives is a process that will go on for the rest of your life. Marriage involves mutually adjusting to each other over and over again. And the more merging and adjusting you are challenged to do before the wedding, the better prepared you will be to continue to adjust to each other after the wedding.

Adjustments you must make include:

- Choosing common goals for the future
- Learning to share responsibility and work together
- Developing a communication system that works
- Learning how to process anger and resolve conflict

Be prepared to accept your personality differences. Are you the spontaneous type while your fiancé likes to plan each detail? Is one of you a neatnik and the other a messy? Or is one a night owl and the other a day lark? Does one live by the clock while the other doesn't care what time it is? Some behaviors can be modified, but basic personality traits usually cannot. If you find areas where you are extremely different, implement one of two strategies. Either learn to accept that fundamental difference and find a way to tolerate it, or develop a mutually agreeable plan for compromise.[1]

As you merge your lives, you need to plan for the future. Besides choosing your color scheme, china, cookware, and filling out those pages and pages of gift registries, you need to talk about and plan where you will live, how you will handle your finances, when to start a family and how to parent, how to relate to friends and relatives, and where to worship.

Understanding each other's past history and present perspective on life's issues will help you adapt to each other in the early months of your marriage. Being willing to adjust to each other and to set goals for your marriage is a lifelong process if you want to continue to grow in intimacy.

Plan Your Wedding

Planning your wedding will no doubt take enormous amounts of your time, energy, and resources. While dozens of excellent resources exist for making this a special day, we have a few general tips that may help you achieve this goal successfully.

First, we suggest you establish boundaries. Weddings are so exciting that everyone wants to get involved. Perhaps circumstances dictate that some family members will be heavily involved in your decision making. Still *you* are the one who must set your own boundaries. You will want to think through what is acceptable and not acceptable in how others relate to you and what decisions will be made by whom. Then do your best to lovingly communicate this to all involved.

Second, try to get all concerned parties on board. With everyone who has some input in the decisions (maybe it's just you or maybe it is four sets of parents and a wedding coordinator!), discuss your dreams, hopes, and preferences right away. Having everyone articulate their ideal of a wedding at the beginning of the process will prevent all sorts of conflicts and stress as the wedding day approaches.

Third, get organized. A wedding planner, a software project management system, or a three-ring binder may be your best friend as you plan your wedding. Having some way to keep track of details, contacts, and to-do lists—no matter how simple or extensive—will make your life easier and reduce your stress. Keep pictures from magazines, price lists, menus, thank-you notes, anything you might need. This not only serves as a resource book, but it will also make a great memento for years to come.

Fourth, don't hesitate to ask for help. We know too many people who tried to single-handedly plan and run their dream wedding. This puts an enormous burden on one person. If you can't hire a professional coordinator, enlist the help of as many friends as possible. Even your parents and their friends might have some special expertise that will come in handy. Bringing in others to help with the wedding preparations will allow you to keep your sanity and enjoy your engagement while it is actually happening.

Be Intentional

This is your engagement! Remember, it is your wedding and your life. Parents, friends, wedding coordinators, caterers, florists, and merchants all want your attention, time, and perhaps even your money! What can you do to accommodate others, get them on board, and encourage them to help you make this a positive time?

Start by evaluating your own expectations. Many couples enter engagement with already stressed family relationships. Sticky issues are best dealt with at the beginning. With so many blended families, you simply must talk about your expectations up front. Understanding each other's expectations will help you be intentional in the way

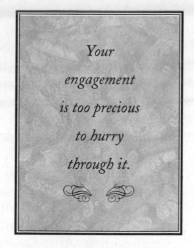

Your

engagement

is too precious

to hurry

through it.

you address them. But ultimately, this is your life, and the choices you make today will influence your life tomorrow.

To be more intentional, each day make a list of things that need to be accomplished. Number them in order of importance. Then intentionally do the most important things on your list first. If you don't complete your list each day, at least you will have taken care of the most important things on it. At the end of the day, transfer those things yet undone to a new list for tomorrow, and start the process all over again. Realizing you can't do it all will help you be more intentional and satisfied with what you *can* do. One of our favorite quotes is "Life is too precious to hurry through it." To become more intentional, you might rephrase this quote to read: "My engagement is too precious to hurry through it."

Have a Stress Action Plan

Stress is inevitable during every engagement; have a specific action plan for keeping it to a minimum. Keep a list of possible stress reducers to pull out as you need them. Here are nine suggestions for relieving stress and for enjoying your engagement:

1. Look for humor and don't take yourself so seriously. At times you will either laugh or cry. Choose to laugh. Twenty-five years from now, you won't remember the little hitches and irritations, and you will laugh about the larger ones.

2. Accept each other. No one is perfect—not you or your fiancé! When under stress, it's easy to become irritated with each other. So be willing to accept those little irritating habits and see them as lovable idiosyncratic behaviors. It is one gift you can give to your future marriage.

3. Have regular dates with your fiancé. Knowing that you will have time alone with each other will help you handle the daily stresses of your engagement. Too often we see engaged couples stop the habit of regular dates. We strongly believe dating is a healthy habit of a rich marriage, so don't slack off now.

4. Keep a journal. Journaling is a great way to manage and reduce stress. After the wedding, it will be fun to read back through the milestones of your engagement. Be sure to record funny happenings as well.

5. Don't take everything relatives and friends say at face value. During times of tension, empathize and give others the benefit of the doubt. Others are also experiencing stress.

6. Cultivate a positive attitude toward your new in-laws-to-be, and get to know them. You'll minimize misunderstandings when you seek to build positive relationships. And in the future, you'll be glad to have them as your friends.

7. Get enough sleep and exercise. Exercising together not only reduces stress, but can start a positive lifelong habit!

8. Eat a well-balanced diet. Starving yourself to drop ten pounds may make you more moody and irritable and hinder your enjoyment of your engagement.

9. Keep perspective. Remember, whatever challenges you must face during your engagement, you will achieve your ultimate goal—after the wedding you will be married!

Build Teamwork and Develop Relational Skills

Marriage is a long-term, lifelong commitment to change, to adjust to each other, and to grow together. To facilitate that process, during your engagement you can develop teamwork skills and begin to grow in your relationship.

Before marriage, we strive to present our best side to each other—to be on our best behavior. Because we are so intent on impressing each other, we don't always realize that those things that attract us to each other before marriage can become irritations after marriage. For instance, Claudia loved Dave's easygoing disposition until we were married and she couldn't get him to move. Before marriage, Dave was

Your ability to pull together instead of push apart will be tested daily.

fascinated with Claudia's endless energy and activities. After marriage, he just wanted one quiet evening at home. We had to learn how to accept and balance our differences and work together as a team.

Make a list of your individual strengths. Then compare your list and see what a great team you make. Begin to affirm how your future spouse's strengths complement and benefit your team. If you are weak in an area in which your fiancé is strong, see this as an asset for your future marriage partnership!

Certainly, planning a wedding and preparing for a marriage will give you numerous opportunities to work together, to surmount obstacles, and to endure stress. Your ability to pull together instead of to push apart will be tested daily. While this process may be stressful, it can be beneficial to your future life together.

Practice Creative Problem Solving

Every engagement comes equipped with its own set of challenges. Making wedding plans and dealing with parents and others offer opportunities to practice creative problem solving.

Remember, problems are "obstacles to growth," and together you can creatively solve them. From choosing your wedding invitations to seating the bridal party, family, and friends at the rehearsal dinner, you have the opportunity to be creative, not get so upset, and avoid escalating whatever the issue is into a major problem. One key to creative problem solving is to remember to attack the problem and not each other. In our own marriage, we've learned to follow three steps to solve problems:

1. *Define the issue or problem to be resolved.* When trying to solve a problem, don't skip the first step, which is to identify the issue! It's futile to debate or try to find a solution when you're not talking about the same thing. You may want to actually write down whatever the issue is. For example, perhaps you are arguing about what items will be included in your buffet line when the real issue is one partner's concern about having the buffet line in the first place. Or maybe one of you has some personal issues to resolve with a divorced parent that keep creeping up when discussing which family will pay for what items.

2. *Brainstorm possible solutions.* Be as creative as you can be. Interject humor when appropriate. The more possibilities you come up with, the greater the chance of finding an appropriate solution.

3. *Choose one solution and try it.* If it doesn't work, go back to your list and choose another possible solution. At this point, if you can't agree, you may want to include another person as a mediator. Sometimes, a friend who is not as emotionally involved can help you be more creative and find a solution that you both can agree to. This principle also works when dealing with parents and others who are involved in planning the wedding.

Basically, with any situation or problem, there are three ways to find a creative solution. One way is to give a gift of love. Maybe the color of the bridesmaids' dresses or the menu for the reception is just not as important to you as it is to your fiancée. You could simply give a gift of love by going along with what your fiancée wants. Second, you can give a gift of individuality and simply agree to disagree. There are some issues you don't have to resolve. Think how boring life would be if you agreed on everything. The third way to find a creative solution is to give a little. Compromise is an important word in every engagement and marriage. So look for ways you can both give a little. It will help your relationship a lot.

Have Couple Times

To stay connected with each other during your engagement, we suggest starting the habit of a "couple sharing time." This is a habit we have had for many years and one we would have started before we were married if we had known how much it would enrich our relationship. Basically a couple sharing time is a regular time when you share your inner thoughts and feelings with each other. Let each partner speak without interruption. Listening is just as important as sharing your own feelings.

A couple sharing time doesn't have to be a large amount of time. Even ten to fifteen minutes a day will help you stay in touch emotionally. If this is not practical—perhaps you don't see each other each day, or have a long-distance relationship—set aside time on a regular basis as often as you can to talk about how you are feeling and anything that has happened to you that you want to share with each other.

A word to the wise: if you must communicate by phone, unless you have unlimited resources, keep track of the time you talk. We know of one engaged couple's monthly phone bills that exceeded two hundred dollars a month. If you have access to e-mail, have couple time through the Internet. Be creative; find ways to stay close during your engagement.

Continue to Woo and Celebrate Each Other

Romancing should not end with the engagement. Just because you are now committed to each other, don't stop wooing and courting. And take time to have some fun. Fun in life is serious business, so plan fun times together with your fiancé. It's easy to get caught up in all the urgent things you must do, but you desperately need times to kick back and just enjoy being together. We're not talking about big blocks of time, but consistent and frequent times of relaxing and having fun. We suggest having at least one planned date each week. Here are some suggestions to get you started:

- Spend an hour together and don't mention the wedding!
- Write a love letter to each other.
- Go to a home improvement store and dream about your future home.
- Have a bookstore date and choose a book to take on your honeymoon.
- Rent the video *Father of the Bride.* There are two versions, one recent and one original with Spencer Tracy and Elizabeth Taylor. We love them both.
- Continue to get to know each other. If there are areas of each other's background or interest you have never discussed, do so now. Inquiring about and getting to know your partner is a great habit to develop as you change and grow throughout your lifetime.

Think of dating and having fun together during your engagement as premarriage vitamins. They are good for your health and will help you stay positive. And you will develop a habit that, over the years, will enrich your marriage.

Get Ready for a Great Marriage

Remember, your wedding is an event; your marriage is a process. Think of your wedding as a vacant lot upon which you will build the house of your marriage. Your engagement is a time for you to gather your building tools and lay the foundation of your life together. By having a great engagement, you will have everything you need to help you build an enriching and healthy marriage.

3

Getting Married Without Drowning in Debt

❧ Ron Blue ❧

The Steve Martin remake of the classic film *Father of the Bride* is one of my favorite movies. Having recently walked the last of my three daughters down the wedding aisle, I can identify with Martin's character and all of the emotions that come with launching your baby into her married life. In my mind, I can still see Martin sitting in his living room amid the postreception debris, marveling over the whirlwind that was his daughter's wedding—and awestruck by the party bill left in the reception's wake.

While the movie was meant to parody the excesses that often accompany a wedding, the fact of the matter is that planning and participating in such a once-in-a-lifetime event can take an incredible toll on emotions, family relationships, and personal finances. The modern wedding industry is a $20 billion-a-year machine, with the average wedding topping out at

You don't have to let wedding bills drown out your wedding bells.

anywhere from $15,000 to $30,000! As the wedding bells get drowned out by wedding bills, my guess is that for many contemporary couples and their parents, Steve Martin's experience looks a lot more like truth than fiction.

But it doesn't have to be that way. My wife, Judy, and I have paid for three weddings in the past several years, and we have emerged with our finances—as well as our family relationships—intact and even strengthened as a result. It doesn't matter whether you plan to pay for your own wedding or your parents have offered to foot all or part of the bill, you can take some definite steps to de-stress the wedding payment process. It *is* possible to get married without drowning in debt—you just have to know how to plan properly.

Set an Upper Limit on What You Are Willing to Spend

Since most of us are relatively inexperienced when it comes to planning or participating in a wedding, the idea of doing it "properly" has an unfamiliar, far-off ring. But when I say you need to know how to plan properly, I am not talking about knowing how to choose flowers, diamonds, or a wedding gown. Instead, I am talking about how you approach the entire wedding process. To financially survive—and even thrive—during the months of planning and preparation for a wedding, you need to remember two words: *Upper Limit.*

Most people never set a maximum on what they are willing to spend on a wedding. They generally have a "hoped for" upper limit, but rarely is it well defined or based on an accurate understanding of what everything will actually cost. When our daughters were still in high school, Judy and I watched some close friends of ours plan their daughter's wedding. The ceremony and reception were lovely, but not extravagant. Knowing what the couple had spent on the total bill, I told our girls we would do the same. We would budget a specific amount of money to pay for their weddings. If they wanted to spend more, they were welcome to use their savings to supplement the wedding budget. If they spent less than the predetermined amount, I offered to let them keep the difference. (Cynthia, our oldest daughter, remembers my telling her she was free to elope, if she wanted to, and keep the entire wedding budget for herself and her husband-to-be!)

> *Instead of feeling constrained by the budget, the girls felt liberated by it.*

Once we had established a spending maximum, Judy and I let the girls decide how the actual dollars would be spent. If special music was important to them, they could have it—so long as they recognized the trade-offs that might be involved. Perhaps they would be willing to use less expensive flowers or ask a friend to videotape the wedding instead of hiring a professional. It didn't matter how they allocated the money; the important thing was that they stayed under our maximum limit.

Instead of feeling constrained by the budget, the girls felt liberated by it. Karen, the youngest of the three, used her discretion to purchase a relatively expensive wedding gown. "I fell in love with it," she admits. "Mom and I had been shopping and shopping for a dress without finding anything I really liked. When the saleslady brought this dress to me and I tried it on I *knew* it was the one—and then I saw the price tag."

Uncertain as to what she should do, Karen showed us the dress. Judy and I agreed that it was perfect. "It's up to you," I told

Karen. "If you love it that much, then get it. That's the freedom you have within your budget."

Karen spent three or four days breaking the anticipated wedding expenses down into smaller budgets to see whether or not she could buy the special gown and still pull off the wedding that she and Mark, her fiancé, wanted to have. She decided it could work, so she went back and bought the dress. Was it worth it? "Definitely," Karen says. "That dress was my favorite part of the whole wedding."

By setting an upper limit on what you will spend on the wedding, your priorities become crystal clear. You force yourself to decide which elements in the wedding budget are necessities and which could be eliminated or scaled back. You can see which things matter the most to you and then use your allowance to ensure that those elements will line up with your vision.

Without a maximum allowance in mind, on the other hand, each of the individual spending decisions becomes a potential trap. You will find yourself asking the very same question about every aspect of the wedding, from the invitations to the flowers to the reception food: *Should you get the ones you like the best, or should you pick whichever option is the least expensive?* Each mini-decision can become an agonizing emotional struggle. But if you take the time to prioritize your needs and desires, you can easily decide where you should economize and where you are free to splurge.

List Your Expenses

In order to prioritize effectively, start with a blank sheet of paper. List everything you expect to spend money on—from invitations and stamps, to church or minister fees, to a wedding trousseau to take along on your honeymoon. (I didn't even know how to spell *trousseau* when our oldest daughter got married, much less what it was or how much it would cost!)

At this point, it will be helpful to consult a wedding planning book or a bridal magazine, available at your local library or bookstore. Such resources usually offer a complete listing of all the expenses and responsibilities associated with a wedding, with general guidelines as to what you might expect to spend. But be prepared to do some of your own research; based on the type of ceremony and reception you want to have, you could wind up paying anywhere from several hundred dollars to multiple tens of thousands for the wedding.

When our girls made their expense lists, they included everything—from the gifts for their bridesmaids to the wedding present Judy and I planned to give them. (I think we even asked the girls what they each wanted us to give them, and then we put it in the total budget.) Your list should reflect the ceremony and reception that *you* want to have—and not just what some bridal magazine thinks is important. When Judy and I got married thirty years ago, we had a small wedding with a reception at the church where we served cake and punch. The entire event cost about $300. That suited us just fine—but you'd never find a wedding like ours showcased in one of today's bridal magazines!

Once you have made your list, total it up. If you can't afford everything without going into debt, start by looking for creative ways to reduce your expenses. Perhaps, instead of hiring a professional photographer, you could ask a friend to take pictures for you. Likewise, your choices on how many guests to invite, what kind of food and drinks to serve, and where to have the reception—at the church, a country club, or someplace else—will make a significant difference in how much everything will cost.

For example, when Judy and I were engaged, she bought her wedding dress from a friend for $25. The friend's wedding had been canceled at the last minute, and Judy wound up with a brand-new, beautiful gown. You can imagine my surprise when, years later, a client told me he had spent $8,000 for his daughter's wedding dress. I didn't even know they made dresses that cost that much!

If you are uncertain about what something will cost, don't be afraid to ask other friends or family members. You might even

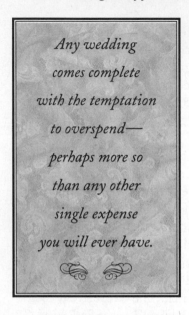

Any wedding comes complete with the temptation to overspend— perhaps more so than any other single expense you will ever have.

need to make a few phone calls. If, for instance, you aren't sure how much money is appropriate to give the minister or the organist for their services, call the church and ask. Remember: *You have never done this before.*

It's also a good idea to round up on all your expenses. Denise, our middle daughter, was the first one to get married. She is very meticulous by nature and did a thorough job (she thought) of researching and estimating her expenses. On paper, it looked as though her wedding expenses would come in way under budget. In reality, though, we pretty much used up every dollar. "I never really wanted an extravagant or expensive wedding," Denise says. "But I was surprised by all the hidden costs. Everything seemed to cost more than the original quote—it's easy to see how people can overspend on a wedding without even realizing it!"

Any wedding comes complete with the temptation to overspend—perhaps more so than any other single expense you will ever have. Because weddings happen only once in a lifetime, it's easy to justify your desires. As with Karen's wedding dress, it's okay to splurge on some things. But if you go overboard on everything, you (or your parents) may find yourself drowning in debt for months—or even years—after the honeymoon is over. To safeguard your finances—and your sanity—set an upper limit and stick to it.

Safeguard Your Relationships

Having survived three weddings (four, when you count my own), I have to agree with the experts who say that getting married is one of the most stressful times in a person's life. Even in situations where there is no apparent conflict or uncertainty, weddings mean change—and that can translate into stress. Figuring out how to successfully pay for everything only adds to an already potent mix of emotions.

During the weeks and months prior to our daughters' weddings, Judy remained remarkably calm. Wondering what she was missing, she finally asked the caterer, who had become a good friend of ours, why people got so stressed out over planning a wedding. "They try to do too much by themselves," came the caterer's instant reply, "or they spend more than they can afford."

By sticking to your predetermined upper limit you can, obviously, eliminate the temptation to overspend and the stress that overspending causes. But even in families and among couples who work within a budget, the wedding process can generate conflict and tension. At the beginning of this chapter I mentioned that our family emerged from each wedding with our relationships both intact and strengthened. The secret to our success, I believe, was that everyone involved in planning the wedding was on the same side of the fence. Everyone, in other words, had the same expectations, the same objectives, and the same understanding of our upper limit.

In order for the parents and the engaged couple to all be on the same side of the fence, several key questions need to be asked and addressed—even before the upper limit begins to take shape: *Whose wedding is it? What are your expectations?* and *Who will pay for what?*

Whose Wedding Is It?

Judy and I may have gotten married for $300, but as she reminds me, times have changed. We have attended some weddings where it seemed like the main point of the party was not to celebrate a couple's marriage, but to make a statement about the net worth of the bride's family!

Such was the case when one of our daughter's friends got married. Her parents hosted a sit-down dinner for five hundred people at a country club, complete with a dance band and an open bar. My guess is that the evening cost about $100,000. It was a lovely party—but nothing like what the bride would have planned, had she been calling the shots.

> *The number one contributor to financial stress surrounding a wedding is the gap between expectations and reality.*
>
> 🐝   🐝

I suspect that in a large majority of the cases where parents pay for all or part of the total wedding bill, the event becomes the parents' party. That's not necessarily wrong—so long as everyone understands the situation up front. Engaged couples need to communicate with each other and with their parents about who will set the standards for the wedding and the reception. Our girls (and their fiancés) knew that even though Judy and I were planning to pay for their wedding, they were free to make their own choices on everything from the guest list to the reception food. Parents need to face reality: Don't pretend it's your daughter's wedding if the event is really going to be *your* party.

What Are Your Expectations?

The number one contributor to financial stress surrounding a wedding is the gap between expectations and reality. Before you set a wedding date, before you draw up a guest list, before you establish an upper limit on your spending, before you do *anything* related to wedding planning, have a meeting between the bride, the groom, and the bride's parents. Ask each participant what he or she wants the wedding to look like. Regardless of who is paying for the wedding, it's a good idea to keep open lines of communication to avoid future disappointments.

A word to engaged couples: If you know something is particularly important to your parents, you would do well to honor your father and mother by working to accommodate their desire. In the Ten Commandments offered in Scripture, only one comes with a promise attached: "Honor your father and your mother, *so that you may live long in the land the LORD your God is giving you*" (Exodus 20:12, emphasis added).

And a word to the parents: If you give your daughter a budget, as Judy and I did, don't impose unfair restrictions or burdens on how the money is used. If, for example, you want to throw a wedding party that includes a sit-down dinner, but your daughter would be content with a buffet, don't force her to factor the expensive dinner into the budget. If it matters that much to you, add an extra allowance to the spending limit to cover the cost.

Who Will Pay for What?

Once you have made a list of all the wedding expenses, decide who will pay for what. Typically, the groom (or his family) pays for the wedding rings, the rehearsal dinner, and the honeymoon. Everything else is the bride's responsibility. (In addition to our daughters, Judy and I have two college-age sons. It will be interesting, when the time comes, to watch a wedding come together from the groom's perspective!)

By deciding, in advance, what everyone—the bride's parents, the groom's parents, the bride, and the groom—will pay for, and by outlining your expectations for the event, you can avoid the emotional power struggles that can sabotage family relationships. When one of Karen's friends got married, Karen watched the bride, her fiancé, and her parents argue back and forth over every single spending decision. First, it was the wedding dress, then the invitations, then the flowers, then the type of reception they wanted to have—and on and on and on. "It really made me appreciate the decision-making freedom I had within our budget," Karen says. "And I think our system saved a lot of the emotional trauma that you often see in weddings—especially between fathers and daughters."

"Happily Ever After" Begins Before "I Do"

Perhaps it was my promise to give my daughters any left-over funds in the wedding budget that motivated them to make their spending decisions with care. Or maybe their budget consciousness stemmed from the fact that they knew Judy and I were footing the bill, and they wanted to demonstrate respect for our generosity. (As Denise put it, "I have never been very big on spending someone else's money.")

Whatever the reason, the girls did a masterful job putting their weddings together on a budget. I am proud of their accomplishments—but even more than that, I am encouraged by what their ability to work within a budget says about their aptitude for handling money in general. I believe you can tell a good deal about a couple's financial future from how they make decisions and spend money during the wedding process.

"Happily Ever After" does not begin with the words "I do." Instead, the training for a successful marriage starts before that, as each individual learns the basic skills that make a marriage work—skills such as how to manage money effectively. Whether you are a parent looking to equip your son or daughter for a financially secure marriage, or whether you want to strengthen your own grasp of financial management, you need to understand and apply four main principles: (1) Spend less than you earn; (2) Avoid debt; (3) Maintain financial liquidity; and (4) Set long-term goals. Until you master these guidelines, financial security will be a far-off and elusive dream.

I have written two financial management books that may help you: *Master Your Money* and *Taming the Money Monster*. *Master Your Money* is a hands-on guide to effective financial management, while *Taming the Money Monster* deals specifically with helping readers conquer debt.

For parents, a wedding is often the last big project they undertake with their daughters. Planning the ceremony and reception should be a positive, enjoyable experience. Nobody wants to get married—or to give a daughter in marriage—with a trail of financial mistakes or broken relationships behind them.

To safeguard your finances—as well as your relationships—plan ahead. Set an upper limit on what you are willing to spend, talk openly with your fiancé and your parents about your expectations, and look for creative ways to make your vision a reality without going into debt. Set yourself up for living "happily ever after" by making the right decisions now, while you are still getting ready for the wedding.

4

What to Do with Wedding Jitters

 Robert and Rosemary Barnes

*I*twas ten in the evening, and there was a knock on the door of our study. The voice on the other side of the door was our daughter, Torrey, asking, "Do you have a minute to talk?" Eighteen-year-old Torrey often used us for her sounding board when she was trying to process something.

She took a seat in the chair next to the desk and asked a question that plagues us all when we are on the verge of significant steps in our lives. "How can I know for sure that this is the right decision?" she asked. "How can I know that this is what I'm supposed to do with my life? I'm just three weeks away from leaving, and I can't seem to deal with these questions and fears that keep popping up."

"Honey," I said to her, "this is a very important decision. You're bound to feel jitters. Right before we got married we had some last-minute fears, if you can believe that. After four years of chasing your mother and getting her to finally accept my proposal, a month away from the wedding I had doubts. Unfortunately, I chose to keep them to myself. I didn't want to cause anyone any panic as they were making all the preparations for the wedding. I thought there must be something wrong with me. How could I want something so much, for so long, and then have doubts?

"Mom, on the other hand, did something about her doubts. Yes, she did have doubts, and that came as no surprise to anyone who knew how different we were! Instead of ignoring her doubts or denying they existed, she found a way to deal with them. She discovered how to decide whether to listen to her doubts or not."

> *A first step in dealing with wedding jitters is to be willing to acknowledge that they are okay to have.*

"If you two had doubts about something as important as getting married," Torrey said as she looked down at the floor of the study, "I guess I don't feel so bad having doubts about college."

Looking Back Is Healthy

A first step in dealing with wedding jitters is to be willing to acknowledge that they are okay to have. Looking back over your shoulder once you've decided upon a course is only natural. But what about those people who get married and never seem to have had any doubts at all? Why is it that some people seem so confident and others seem plagued with doubts?

Some people make decisions totally on emotion. They get their adrenaline running to such a high pitch that they don't ever stop to analyze what they are doing. For the person who makes decisions based on feelings alone, a time will come when they will have to deal with their doubts—usually shortly after the wedding, when the honeymoon is over.

Other people have doubts concerning their impending wedding, but choose not to talk about them. Some feel guilty that they could even have any apprehensions at all. "After all," one young man said, "look at all the things everyone is doing to make this such a special wedding. With all that's being done for me here, how could I question this decision to get married?"

It's important to allow the doubts to surface. Having questions and pre-wedding jitters is very natural. Most people have pre-wedding apprehensions, and these jitters fulfill a very helpful function. Marriage is a life-changing decision. Our emotions play a very dramatic part in this life-changing decision. Doubts offer an opportunity to cut through the vapor of the emotion of the wedding, allowing you to analyze for yourself where the marriage is taking you and with whom it is taking you there.

When a person finds himself looking back over his shoulder or developing cold feet about a wedding, it's time to locate the focal point of the jitters. Most often, our jitters tend to focus on one or more of the following questions:

Who am I, and am I ready to commit to marriage?
What will the commitment of marriage do to alter my life?
Who is this person I am getting ready to marry?

In other words, these three questions ask: (1) Is it about me? (2) Is it about marriage? or (3) Is it about my future spouse? The difficulty of these very deep questions may cause you to get extreme jitters. Good for you! You're thinking! It's healthy to ask these questions. Now let's look at each of those questions in more detail.

Is It About Me?

As our daughter Torrey started dealing with her jitters about leaving home and going off to college a thousand miles away from home, she discovered something she hadn't expected. After taking an extended college tour more than a year earlier, Torrey and her mother had such an incredible peace about this one particular college that she decided not to even apply to any other schools. The college of her choice accepted her before her senior year of high school even started. The school offered everything she had wanted and prayed for. It was obvious to all of us that she had made the correct choice. Then why the doubt? She finally realized that it wasn't the college that she was doubting. Instead, she doubted herself. Was she ready, at this particular time in her life, to go so far away to school? Just as Torrey's doubts had nothing to do with her choice of a college, some people's pre-wedding jitters really have nothing to do with their fiancé.

"I finally realized," Brian said to his counselor, "it's not Linda that I have these doubts about, it's really me." Brian had come in alone for premarriage counseling with a written list of things about Linda that were causing him concern. Even though Brian had written them down, his counselor wrote them on a portable blackboard so that they could look at them together. Standing there, Brian finally realized what his counselor had already surmised. This young man discovered that it wasn't his fiancée that was causing him the jitters, it was his own readiness.

Marriage is a huge step. It's not an additive to your life's agenda—an agenda that you have already set in place and will attempt to work a marriage into. Marriage is an alternative to living the way a person lives before the wedding. Yes, it is a huge decision, and people should take it far more seriously than they do. For marriage is a dramatic step away from singleness.

For some people, the first question is what causes them to look back over their shoulders. Are they personally ready for such a commitment? "But who's ready!" Brian blurted out. "I know in my heart that I love Linda. Were you ready to get married before you got married?" he asked his counselor with tremendous frustration and fear in his voice.

His counselor tried to answer. "No one is really ready," he said. "It's a commitment to spend the next fifty years getting more and more ready each day. A willingness to commit to read, talk, and ask questions, so you can learn more about being married."

Is It About Marriage?

How will marriage alter my life? And am I ready for those changes? Those are difficult questions to answer objectively. Most of the dreams that God has placed in a person's heart include a spouse. Dreams of one's own family. Dreams of companionship. Dreams of pursuing a particular direction in life such as a career, profession, or ministry.

The self-centered stage of singleness often makes it difficult to imagine blending or even curtailing those dreams for the dreams that another person might have. But marriage means just that. It means two people with two distinct sets of dreams becoming a single team that is heading in one direction.

Sounds scary and perhaps, for some, it sounds too sacrificial. Yet that's the beauty of the marriage process. Two people working together can complete each other.

We got married in 1972. We could not have been more different in the way we looked at things. In fact, we were opposites in almost every way. One of us is a night person, while the other is an early morning person. That pretty much typifies the way we look at everything. Everything, that is, with the exception of two very crucial areas. We both had and still have a strong commitment to Christ and a strong commitment to our marriage.

Some people wonder how getting married will impact their own personal wants or desires. Will they individually get what they want after they get married? They got much of what they wanted in life when they were single. Will getting married change all that?

This self-centered outlook will cause great pre-wedding jitters. "Will I still get what I want after the wedding?" The correct outlook is not that *I got married*, but that *I am married*.

"I am married" means that I will go into the marriage questing to blend rather than win. The wedding is not just a ceremony where a person gets married. It's the beginning of a quest. Questing to share ideas rather than get my way. After a period of adjustment in our own marriage, we decided to be married.

It was then that God gave us dreams greater than we could have ever thought of on our own. Our differences were our strengths. We were both able to see things differently and, therefore, be much stronger as a team. In short, deciding *to be married* and blending, gave us greater happiness than we could have ever found alone.

Is It About Your Future Spouse?

Fewer things can cause more stress on a young couple than the preparation for a wedding. The logistical decisions that need to be made for a wedding will bring out in neon lights the personality quirks and character flaws not only of our future spouse, but of our future in-laws as well. The tension of wedding preparations can cause engaged individuals to think they must have been blind to some of the things they now see in their fiancé. When people date, they often only see perfection in the other person. As a wedding looms on the horizon, those perfections begin to wear thin.

Everyone needs the right to be human. Imperfections are a reality of life, even if they are a shock when revealed in the one you love. Again, it's healthy to see those imperfections for what they are. Just imperfections or immaturities. We all have them. The finishing school of years in the marriage process seems to be one of God's ways of sanding those imperfect rough edges.

Diane sat on the porch with her uncle, her head in her hands. It was just two months before the wedding, and her fiancé, Billy, was starting to show his rough edges. Billy just didn't want to do most of the wedding ceremony traditions that she and her mother had always dreamed of. Each time Diane and Billy talked about the ceremony and reception, his standard response was, "I don't want to do that . . . do we have to do all that? Let's just get married. Why make it such a show?" It had gotten to the point where they couldn't even be civil about their own wedding.

"He seems so different, Uncle Jack," she sighed.

"What do you mean by different?" her uncle asked.

"Oh, Billy is so argumentative and doesn't want to do anything I want to do. For the first time, I'm having real doubts. He seems so immature. Doesn't he understand that this is our *wedding?* It's not just some party we're having!" She burst into tears.

"No," her uncle answered after waiting a moment, "he probably doesn't understand your view of what the wedding should be. How can he? He's not you." Diane's uncle then went on to describe all the problems he had caused at his own wedding many years ago. Thirty years after the fact it was a hilarious story .

"You did that, Uncle Jack? And Aunt Lisa went on to marry you anyway?" Diane asked incredulously.

"Oh, she just knew I was immature and insecure," Uncle Jack said. "The way I dealt with my insecurities was to make fun of everyone and cause problems."

Different people respond to stress in different ways, especially when they are young and feeling nervous. Yes, Billy was immature, but Lisa was equally immature in her approach to him, because she expected perfection from an imperfect, unfinished person.

On the road of life there are red flags that indicate you can keep driving, but be aware of some hazards. These road signs say "Stop" and look both ways before proceeding any further. Red flags are warning signs that should be observed carefully. Ongoing arguments during the wedding preparation, as well as other hurt feelings and immaturities brought out as the pressures of the wedding approach, are signals that say this marriage could be difficult, but you may proceed with caution.

Road Closed

Other young people encounter problems that are not so easily dismissed. These concerns are not so much insecurities or minor immaturities as they are serious character flaws. I call these character flaws "road closed" signs.

Weeks before her wedding, Laury found that her fiancé had spent the night with another woman. When confronted by her friends with this obvious road closed sign, her response was, "Well, technically we're not really married yet."

Infidelity happening just weeks before a wedding indicates that the road needs to be closed until further notice. When signs of a lack of honesty or integrity appear, it's time to stop the car. Other "road closed" signs would include physical or verbal abuse, alcoholism, drug addiction, gambling, major religious differences, chronic lying, and so on.

How does a person distinguish red flags from road closed signs? In the heat and fear of the moment, many problems may make it look like it's time to close the road, when actually the couple merely needs to slow down and look at the marriage more seriously and rationally, rather than emotionally. Other people, however, can get so blinded that they are willing to drive right off the cliff, even when their friends and family are screaming for them to stop the car. The best way to distinguish between a red flag and a road closed sign is to get objective glasses.

Get Objective Glasses

If you are having doubts about your marriage, listen to your friends and family, and seek the advice of someone you trust.

Laury, the woman whose boyfriend cheated on her, discounted the opinions of those who knew her best. When her closest friends started warning her against marriage, rather than weighing their concerns, she discontinued her relationship with them. Laury then became very isolated. She also lost out on receiving all the input her friends had to offer. She was on a dangerous road.

Todd was engaged to a girl he had dated for a long time. As the wedding date neared, he was suffering from all the standard pre-wedding jitters. His problem wasn't so much the fears, but how he was dealing with those fears. Instead of choosing one or two trusted people to discuss his fears with, he talked with everyone who would listen—friends, coworkers, and church acquaintances. Not only did he receive a wide variety of advice, but soon the entire world around him knew about his doubts. Soon, word of his doubts got back to his fiancée and her family. This was not only an insult to his fiancée, but it put a tremendous damper on the pre-wedding excitement for all who were involved. Although Todd had expressed concerns about his fiancée's maturity, it was actually Todd's immaturity that was causing the problem. He was gaining a lot of attention for his whining.

Pick one or two trusted people to discuss your doubts with. We all have doubts; they will not be surprised at yours. They need to be trustworthy to keep your questions confidential, as well as trusted for their concern for you and your future. In addition, they need to be objective and wise. Can they give godly advice? Can they be objective as they look at your concerns? Many parents can be objective. Other parents think that no one is good enough to marry their child. Advice from that parent will be tainted.

Take the opportunity to look at the red flags through another person's glasses. Another set of "eyes" might be able to see things a little bit more clearly. You may be so emotionally wrapped up in the relationship that you are blind to things taking place right in front of you. Another view is very helpful.

Parents, one or two trusted friends, a relative or pastor, or even a counselor can supply this view. When doubts keep popping up, neither ignore them, nor respond with a knee-jerk reaction by canceling everything. Get a second opinion, but make sure the person offering the advice has the right motive in mind. Make sure their glasses are clean.

Most Red Flags Mean Check to See How You're Driving

It's one thing to ask for advice. It's yet another to be willing to take that advice. Most of the time that advice will be just an explanation that pre-wedding jitters are normal and even healthy. We all have to grow up and understand that fallible humans marry other fallible humans. No one is perfect.

But on those rare occasions when you encounter a sign that says "stop the car, this road is closed," you have to choose. You can choose to ignore the sign and drive off the end of a cliff, or you can take a very serious look at whether to continue with the wedding or not. Ask yourself the question: "What's causing these jitters? Is it my own unreadiness, my fear of marriage, or my unrealistic view of my fiancé? Is there something much deeper here?" Get some help in answering those questions. Generally the problem will boil down to little more than a road you thought was going to be perfect but instead has a few bumps along the way. In that case, the destination is certainly worth making the journey.

5

Enjoying the Wedding of Your Dreams

❧ David and Jan Stoop ❧

*Y*ou know from listening to your married friends that a wedding day can be a nightmare, or it can be a dream-come-true. What makes the difference? In interviewing a number of newly married brides, one thing became very clear: The differences between a dream and a nightmare were things that were in the hands of the couple-to-be—things they could have controlled.

Don and Marcie are a prime example: "We're so thankful we have a video of our wedding; I don't remember anything—it was all a blur," states Marcie. "I worked so hard on the details that by the day of the wedding, I was a nervous wreck!"

Don agreed and took some of the blame. "I didn't realize how much there was to a wedding, at least for the type of wedding Marcie had dreamed of having. So I wasn't much help. I figured weddings are for the brides—my part was to just show up on time."

"In fact," Marcie added, "I think I set myself up. I can remember saying to Don a couple of months before the wedding that it was to be my special day, and all he had to worry about was being there. And being there on time, of course!" Then Marcie added, almost as an afterthought, "I wish we had done it differently. I wish I had involved Don more and delegated a whole lot more to other people."

Don continued, "I wish we both had done things differently. I know that Marcie just tried to do too much, and I stood by and let her.

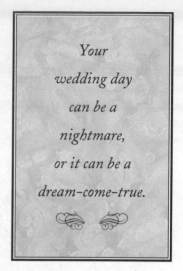

Your wedding day can be a nightmare, or it can be a dream-come-true.

Even with her friends and family helping her, there were just too many bases for her to cover. She drove herself crazy trying to keep everything under control. What I didn't realize early enough was that I was helping create a frazzled, exhausted bride!"

Or listen to John and Kimberly.

"We almost called the whole thing off," Kimberly said. Then she quickly added, "But I'm glad we didn't. I sure wish someone had coached us, though, through the process."

John described the months before the wedding. "I started to avoid being with Kimberly. She was a mess. Everything became an issue—the colors of the bridesmaids' dresses, the color of her mother's dress, what my groomsmen were going to wear, and even the vows we were going to say. We fought over whether we should write our own, memorize them, or repeat them after the minister. I think we both questioned our sanity a number of times during those weeks. But we continued to pressure each other and somewhat reluctantly pressed ahead with the wedding."

"I think I got caught up in trying to make *all* my dreams come true," Kimberly continued. "The day had to be perfect! So every time I thought of something else that could be part of the day, I had to add it. For example, we went to a friend's wedding, and they had mints wrapped in lace with a scroll that contained a personal message from the bride and groom. I thought it was beautiful, and of course I wanted it in our wedding, too. Only mine had to be hand-done in calligraphy, not simply printed. I don't even know how we got them finished. Looking back now, it wasn't really that important. But that wasn't what I felt then. Back then I thought it was absolutely essential no matter how many nights I went without sleep."

"It was awful," John said, "and I know Kim agrees. There were several times when I suggested we just run off to Vegas and get married. We almost did one time. If we had, we might have gotten a better start in our relationship."

On the other hand, listen to Pam and Rick.

"We have such great memories," Rick exclaimed. "What a special day!"

"Yeah, but we worked hard to make it that way," Pam quickly added.

"How?" we asked.

"Well," Pam continued, "I think part of it has to do with our personalities. We're both very organized. So, early in the process, we sat down together and made up a chart."

Pam was almost embarrassed when we asked her to explain.

"It's something we do at work. When we have a big project, we first define each of the components, and then lay them out in a time line. It's fun to do."

As Pam talked, Rick went to get their chart from their files. He showed it proudly. Every aspect of the wedding had been laid out on an individual time line with everything converging on the wedding day. There was even a time line for the lace-wrapped mints with the personal message scroll.

As we looked at the chart, one of the things we saw was the obvious—invitations. The time line started with the visit to the different stores where they could order invitations. Then there was a mark at the deadline for ordering the invitation, another mark for picking up the invitations, and a final mark for when they had to be mailed. Written in at each mark was the name of the person who would be responsible for doing that particular task. Rick and Pam's names were by the visits to the stores, also by the ordering notation. Rick's name was by the note to pick them up, and Pam and her sister's and mother's names were noted by the mailing notation.

"What if something came up that wasn't on your chart?" we asked.

"We had several things that came up which we hadn't considered ahead of time," Rick answered. "What we did was sit down together and look at our chart and see if we both felt it was possible. If we agreed, we added it to the chart and assigned responsibility to someone. I know we did that on one thing that came up, and on two other ideas, we both felt we couldn't comfortably do it, and so we dropped the ideas."

"What's this item here about breakfast on the wedding day?" we asked.

"Oh, that was really special," Pam responded. "We didn't agree with the old superstition, or maybe it's just a tradition, that the bride and groom aren't to see each other on the wedding day before the wedding. So we carved out some time on the morning of the wedding to be together. We went out for breakfast, and then had devotions together sitting on the cliff overlooking the beach."

As they looked at each other with that shared memory, it was clear that their wedding day had been a dream-come-true. But then, it should have been for a couple that organized! Does that mean that only those who are good at organizing can truly enjoy their wedding day? No. But personality does enter into how we are going to experience our wedding day. We noted this as we talked with several new wives whom we had known for years. They seemed to fall into two different personality types.

A Tale of Two Personalities

One type is naturally organized, like Pam and Rick. For people like them, finishing a task is of primary importance. They are typically decisive and orderly about their lives.

These people often have such a strong work ethic that they cannot find freedom to play until the job is done. They make quick decisions and then stick by them, even if the decision wasn't the best one they could have made. The problem is, this type of personality can create a nightmare wedding as well. Once they make a decision about some wedding detail, they can sometimes drive themselves to the point of sickness or exhaustion trying to do everything they set out to do.

These people are also naturally good at organizing other people. They are very clear in their instructions, and just seem to know when to check on how others are doing with the task given to them. They like to make lists, and one of their greatest joys in life is crossing something they have finished off their list.

But there is the other type as well, who do not seem to value decisiveness, preferring to put off decisions until the last minute. It is not that they are procrastinating, although they have probably been accused of that. They are usually just hoping for some additional information that will help them make a better decision. So decisions are usually made at the last minute, and even then they are uncomfortable with the correctness of their decision. You can imagine what can happen when a highly organized person marries this type of person. Or when this type of person has a mother who is highly organized!

Their strengths are not found in their organized approach to life, but are seen more in their adaptability and flexibility. They have a play ethic that often makes them fun to be around. To others, it appears they often do things by the seat of their pants. The truth is, all of their lives they have been preparing in some way for that event. They also have a tendency to try to do too much and often end up feeling overwhelmed, especially with something as complex as a wedding. By the time the wedding day arrives, they may finally realize just how much is still left to be done. It would seem that they are more prone to the "blur of anxiety" syndrome on their wedding day, but that is not necessarily the case.

Consider Wayne and Judy. When asked about their wedding, they both said almost in unison, "We had a great day!"

Judy added, "I don't think I've ever had so much fun. It was a celebration in every sense of the word."

"Tell us why," we asked.

"I don't know," replied Wayne, "I think we just planned it that way."

"How did you plan?" we asked, still trying to get some details.

Judy thought a while and then said, "I think part of it was the fact that it was important to both of us that it be a fun day. That was one of our goals. Another reason it was so much fun was that we planned the major events of the wedding together. And then, I simply let my mother do some of the things she thought were important. I remember saying to her, 'If you want that to be part of the wedding, it's okay with me, but you do it.' And she did. She planned a very special thing with Wayne's mom to do with the unity candle. We didn't even know about it until the rehearsal."

"Another reason we had such a fun day," Wayne added, "was that at one point, we stopped planning. We agreed there was only so much we could do. For us, seeing our ceremony as a celebration with all of our friends participating in some way was far more important to us than some of the little details. I guess you could say we decided not to sweat the details."

So how do you make your wedding day a celebration—a dream-come-true, rather than the nightmare that many brides and grooms unfortunately experience? Let's look at eight things a couple can do to make their wedding day more than just a ceremony—something you experience that day, not just an event to be captured on video and experienced later.

Share the Planning

Our talks with couples demonstrated how important it was that the planning of the wedding be something shared between the bride *and* the groom. If the planning of the wedding is important only to the bride, that couple has already set a bad precedent for their relationship. If the wedding is "her thing," then you are going to have to work extra hard down the road to define what is going to be "our thing."

The planning of the wedding needs to be shared between the bride and the groom.

As we listened to the different attitudes couples had about their wedding, we saw a clear correlation between the attitude that the wedding was "our thing" and the quality of their marriage relationship soon after the wedding. This attitude is so important that it might be fair to say: If he is not interested in helping plan the wedding, maybe he is not ready to get married.

Quite often, men pride themselves on not being interested in "women's things," like weddings. This is a typical adolescent attitude that does not bode well for a shared marriage relationship. A man needs to grow beyond such an attitude. He may still think the wedding ceremony is more important to his fiancée, but because it is important to her, it should also be important to him.

A wedding ceremony is a rite of passage, a special event that marks an end to one phase of life and the beginning of another. Our culture typically does not give enough importance to the rites of passage in our adult growth and development. Our lives are enriched when we seek to not only understand the importance of these events, but to also enter into the event in a way that signifies its relevance to our lives. That means both bride and groom need to be involved in this very special rite in order to experience it as the beginning of the next phase in their lives.

Share Your Dreams

The discussion of wedding plans needs to go beyond agreement as to the mutual importance of the wedding day to each partner. It is one thing to say, "Yes, it is important to me," but another to be specifically involved in expressing your desires and listening to your partner express his or her desires. You need to discuss together what you wish the day will be like. You do not have to limit your discussion to the day—talk about the months of preparation, and especially about the whole week leading up to the wedding day. What are some of the important things each of you wishes to do and experience? Talk about it.

Set aside some time for both of you to share your private dreams of how you've always imagined your wedding day.

Think about the wedding day itself. Perhaps you do not agree with Rick and Pam. You may not want to see each other on the wedding day until that moment when the bride makes her appearance at the back of the church. Talk about other things you could do to let each other know how important they are to you *on* your wedding day.

In other words, set some goals. Goals will become clear as you share your dream of your wedding day with each other. Dreams are always the foundation of our expectations. When our dreams are not expressed, our expectations can become a very real problem. Often, our dreams are very real to us. They are so real to us that we think the other person must already know the details. It's hard to remember that if we have not talked about them clearly, the other person will not know the details. So, early in the planning stage, set aside some time for both of you to share your private dreams of how you've always imagined your wedding day.

Once you've each shared your dreams and expectations, take some time to write down each of the specifics in your shared dreams. Then commit to each other that you will follow through on what you have discussed.

Include some downtime—a relaxed time—for you to be together. All too often, couples become lost, cut off from each other, both during the preparations for the wedding, as well as on their wedding day. Don't let that happen to you.

Delegate Early

Responsibilities delegated early in the process are less likely to become problems at the last minute. One way to guarantee that your wedding day will be a blur of anxiety and a time of total fatigue is to try to do it all yourself. This is a day to be shared, not only with your partner-to-be, but with your family and friends. Bridesmaids and groomsmen are there to help. Begin to depend on them early in the process.

If you have done a good job in step two, you probably have been able to identify most of the things that need to be done in preparation for the wedding. As you and your partner-to-be talk about these specific tasks, talk together about who could best help you do them.

When our youngest son got married, his wife-to-be was finishing her next-to-last semester in law school, which was about a thousand miles away from where the wedding was taking place. In addition, her family now lived on the East Coast, and the wedding was to be held on the West Coast. Needless to say, many of the things that needed to be done for the wedding had to be delegated. And she did a great job. Here are the three rules she followed as she delegated different tasks.

First, she gave people not only the responsibility, but the authority to act as well. She helped pick out the invitations, but someone else was responsible for picking them up and for getting them mailed.

Second, she checked up with those to whom she had delegated tasks. She didn't assume that they would automatically take care of everything. She did this several times over the course of preparing for the wedding, but she didn't check so much that she might as well have done it herself.

Third, she let go of what could not be done, or what was messed up by someone else. Fortunately, she did a good job delegating, but there were a few things that slipped through the cracks. Rather than panic and create a "blur of anxiety" on her wedding day, she *let it go*.

Learn to Say No

One of the major things I found that created the blur of anxiety on the wedding day was the omnipotent feeling that one person can do everything. You cannot, and you really do not need to. One newlywed wife said that she had tried to do in her wedding everything she had ever seen and liked in other weddings. Her ceremony lasted over an hour, which meant that some people had been sitting there almost two hours. Now, in looking back, she said, "I wished I could have said *no* to myself. I tried to include so many things only to end up feeling like nothing was really special."

Perhaps the hardest person to say *no* to will be you. The time to do this is when you and your partner-to-be are discussing the wedding day and deciding what to do and what not to do. Once you have done this, you need to discuss together anything you wish to add, making certain that whatever you add is important to *both* of you, and that it is still doable.

Listen to Your Mother

I found that it was important to let the mothers do what they wanted—to a point! Probably the second hardest person to say no to will be the mothers, especially your own. Maybe she's the hardest one to say no to. In fact, she may not even hear your no. One new wife commented, "I think I realized about a month before the wedding that my mother was trying to make this 'her' wedding. She had stopped listening to me and was making decisions on her own, and I hadn't given her the okay to make those decisions."

This woman handled the situation wisely. She went on to say, "Since my mother stopped listening to me, I started to really listen to her. Most of the things she was planning were not a problem to me, but a few were. That was when I had to really make an effort in deciding what was not so important to just let her do it. And I told her so. But on the few things I had to say a strong no to I had to make certain she heard me."

What this young woman illustrated was the ability to let her mother do her thing as long as it didn't cross over the line and interfere with something important to her as the bride. Even though everyone says, "It's *your* wedding!" it is also a landmark event in the life of both sets of parents. It's not worth spoiling the day by alienating a parent or two.

One couple was still trying years later to repair the damage that was done to the wife's mother before the wedding. "We went through the whole day without my mother speaking to me. I'm surprised she even came to the wedding," this wife told us. Unfortunately, she had tried to resolve a lifetime of mother being in control in the weeks preceding the wedding. Again, if you and your partner-to-be have discussed what is really important to both of you, you will know when to say a firm no to a parent, and when to let it ride.

Celebrate the Whole Event

Make your reception a time of celebration as well. The reception is really part of the ceremony, so let's talk about how you can enjoy having to talk to everyone and their brother. The couples who had paced themselves during the earlier part of their wedding day were consistently able to enjoy the reception. Those couples whose memory of the wedding ceremony was only a blur were most often overly tired and unable to enjoy the reception.

Your reception can be a major part of your day's celebration if you have an attitude of celebrating. I noticed that couples who enjoyed the reception were couples where both bride and groom considered the reception to be important. To most of these couples, it was the opportunity to share the day with friends and family.

It's good to plan what you are going to do with your guests at the reception. If you're going to have tables, make it a point to visit with people at each table. No tables? Then plan to mingle with the crowd and make it a point to talk briefly with as many people as possible. Time after time, what couples commented on was how important it was to them later to have spoken with as many people as possible. In the midst of a very special, personal day, these couples shared themselves with those who loved them.

Build Memories

Video is a must! Not only because you have a record of the day, but also because you now have something that can become a part of your anniversary celebrations for years to come. Use it to reaffirm your vows, to check your attitudes towards each other, and to remind yourselves of those special dreams and hopes you held that special day.

I know in our family one of the best parts of the wedding video are the spontaneous, impromptu interviews the photographer did during the reception with as many people as possible. Have the photographer ask people to give you advice. The editor will probably cut out the repetitions, but some people can say the craziest things—things you will want to hear again and again.

Take some time as soon as possible after the honeymoon to view the video alone together. Let it refresh your memory of that day's celebration. Then make a commitment to each other that every year, on your anniversary, no matter what, you will take the time to view it again. Renew your vows to each other as you watch. Notice how much younger you looked each anniversary viewing. When you have children, let them view it with you so they will know the foundation you laid together for the establishment of your family.

Make It a Special Night

While I was interviewing one new wife, she shared something of the greatest importance in making your wedding more than a ceremony. She told me, "I think one of the most important things about making my wedding day more than just a ceremony was the fact that both my husband and I were still virgins. We not only had all of the special things to anticipate during our wedding day, we had the excitement of finally being able to fully respond to each other physically. It added to the anticipation of the day, and our wedding night also added so much to the meaning of our wedding day." Wise words from a young woman who married when she was twenty-five.

Couples who live together before they are married, or who sleep together before they are married, lose the opportunity to experience this special meaning for their wedding day. Some of the couples who had not refrained from sleeping together before their wedding started to understand the importance of what they had lost by not waiting. Several expressed to me how, as the wedding approached, they quit sleeping together just so they could experience some degree of newness in their relationship on their wedding night.

Perhaps this is a good point to remind each other that not only do we want the day and its events to be special, we want to have an attitude that seeks to communicate to the soon-to-be partner their unique specialness to us. Keep this in mind during the planning stages, make it central in your thoughts and attitudes on the wedding day, but most of all, communicate the specialness of the other person to them on your wedding night.

The choice is yours—a dream or a nightmare. You can make your wedding more than a ceremony. Make it your dream-come-true!

How to Have a Great Wedding Night

⤜ Clifford and Joyce Penner ⤛

As you drive away brushing the remaining vestiges of rice and birdseed from your hair and clothing, your mind can't help but jump ahead to the next major event: the wedding night. You reach for each other's hands with that mix of excitement and a touch of apprehension—eager, yet wondering.

It is in the sexual experience that we have the possibility of reaching the highest peaks of ecstasy. Because of the powerful potential of sex, the wedding night is an anniversary event, the significant turning point in every couple's relationship. What happens between the two of you that night will be imprinted on your memory forever. In those moments all by yourselves, after the many days of preparation and anticipation, you are free to abandon all previous restrictions. You can relinquish all physical boundaries. Whether or not this is your first sexual intercourse experience, you can take specific steps to make the first time after your wedding an event associated with positive lasting memories. There are some basic criteria to a "successful" wedding night for every bridal couple.

Are Your Expectations Realistic?

A fulfilling married sexual life is in part dependent on its start. Many couples have a hard time transferring their premarital passion into their marriages because they have false expectations about married sex, they lack information, or they have not communicated openly about their expectations for their wedding night.

Even though you may not have thought about it, you probably have a picture of your ideal sexual experience. What do you envision happening between the two of you and inside each of you during deeply satisfying lovemaking? When do you expect to have your first sexual time together on your honeymoon? Do you imagine that experience will lead to intercourse? How do you feel about that event?

Here are a few suggestions for aligning your expectations for your wedding night with reality.

Carefully Define Success

If your only expectation for your wedding night is that you both enjoy being together without any demands to do more than the most hesitant of your desires, then you will surely succeed and have no regrets. Many first nights are made less than ideal by comparison with some external standard, but if you don't set such a standard, your wedding night can be ideal for you. Set your own standards. Discuss frankly with your fiancé what you feel you will be able to handle that first night. Then don't pressure yourself—or each other—to do more than you are comfortable with.

Plan Your Timing

Think through the wedding, the reception, the time you anticipate leaving the reception, and your expected arrival time at the place you will spend the night. Then add an hour or two because everything usually takes longer than you expect. If you will be leaving the first-night hotel to travel to a different location for the rest of your honeymoon, what time do you have to check out of the hotel? Do you have to catch a flight the next day? Can you extend your checkout time or find a late-enough flight time so that your first night together is not rushed? We recommend you allow at least twelve hours between arrival at the hotel and your departure.

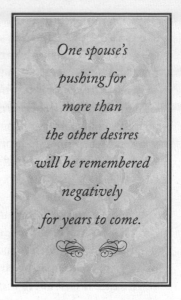

One spouse's pushing for more than the other desires will be remembered negatively for years to come.

Allow Time for Connection

Allow for emotional and spiritual connection. This is often more important for the woman than it is for the man. The wife may be eager to talk through all the details of the wedding and reception. She needs to feel valued as a person. She needs to know her husband responds to her beauty. We were taught that we were to start our first sexual intercourse with a time of Bible reading and prayer. That can be a very important way to connect and invite God into your married sex life. We actually were rather legalistic about that "rule," so Joyce read a passage to Cliff in the car on the way to the motel, and we prayed as we drove. We were both very eager!

Pursue Pleasure, Not Sex

Allow for pleasure without any goal-oriented demands. Remember lovemaking is just that. It is a time of delighting in your bodies without any need for arousal, orgasm, or intercourse. You may want to prepare your bodies and then just enjoy falling asleep in each other's arms. You may enjoy a time of passionate kissing and fondling and then fall asleep and continue later that night or in the morning when you wake up. Or you may enjoy the pleasure of each other's body and a full sexual experience.

What is most important is that you don't go further than both of you desire. Let the most tired, conservative, or hesitant one set the pace and the boundaries. One spouse's pushing for more than the other desires will be remembered negatively for years to come. The consequences are not worth getting what you want at that moment! Limit sexual activity the first night to what both of you would freely desire.

Follow a Great Model

The Song of Songs is the most beautiful model of a wedding night's first sexual experience. Joseph Dillow's book *Solomon on Sex* vividly interprets that Scripture.[1]

Dillow assumes by the text that the bride and groom retire to the bridal chambers around twilight. Solomon begins their time together by raving on and on about the beauty of his wife. His enjoyment of her body is evident—not as a means to his own gratification, but as a deep appreciation of her. Solomon mentions her eyes, hair, teeth, lips, and neck, and he praises her body separately from a sexual focus. It would seem that he is enjoying caressing those parts as he fondly talks about them.

Solomon has connected with his new wife's personhood before he delights in the rest of her body. He uses beautiful symbolism to describe her breasts and nipples. It is clear that he not only enjoys the appearance of her breasts, but he also "feeds" among them. He refers to her genitals as a garden. The frankincense, or scent, of her genitals arouses him. A woman needs to know that her body arouses her husband, especially if her body can be enjoyed for his pleasure without any demand being placed on her. Solomon concludes his response to his bride's body with these words: "All beautiful you are, my darling; there is no flaw in you" (Song of Songs 4:7).

After Solomon affirms her beauty, he creates a fantasy for her of their traveling to her home to make love in the countryside. His excitement builds with intensity as he talks about his heart beating fast, her garden, or genitals, being locked up (those of a virgin), and their genital secretions (symbolically referred to as streams of water and a cistern of water) flowing.

Just as we recommend that the wife initiate entry, the Shulamite invites genital contact (often interpreted as an invitation for oral sex). "Let my lover come into his garden and taste its choice fruits" (Song of Songs 4:16). Never does he seem to push himself on her or demand from her. He just affirms and enjoys her until she begs him to come to her genitals. They consummate their relationship as they eat and drink in the sexual pleasure of one another's body. What a beautiful model God has given us for the sexual relationship between a husband and wife!

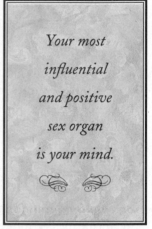

Your most influential and positive sex organ is your mind.

Prepare Your Mind, Spirit, and Soul

We have often said that your most influential and positive sex organ is your mind: it controls your body, how you think about sex, how you feel about sex, and how your body responds to sex. Your beliefs and attitudes about sex were formulated during your growing-up years and will affect what you bring to your sexual relationship in marriage.

Who you are today as a sexual person depends on how successfully you learned about your sexuality at each stage of development. It also depends on the modeling of interaction that took place between you and your parents. From your same-sex parent you learned what it was to be male or female. If your same-sex parent seemed secure and content with his or her sexuality, so will you be. From your opposite-sex parent, you learned how to relate to the opposite sex. If you were affirmed and respected by your opposite-sex parent, you will expect affirmation and respect from your spouse.

Take time to know yourself. Learn whether or not you bring to your sexual relationship in marriage the capacity for intimacy. Determine if you have a naturalness in giving and receiving affection, a comfortableness with your body, an awareness of your sexuality, a high view of the sexual relationship in marriage as a mutual commitment, and a confidence that you can make sexual pleasure happen.

Carve out time to nurture your own personal inner self, your relationship with God, and your relationship with each other. Make certain you take time to keep your spirits and souls fed. If you come to the wedding and honeymoon totally depleted, you will have nothing to give and may even have difficulty receiving.

To keep your spirits connected, you might share a brief daily or weekly Bible reading or prayer time together. Also, frequent walks and talks can help relieve stress and keep you connected.

The day of the wedding is most critical. Plan your day so that you can sleep in as long as your body will allow you (unless you have a morning wedding). The rest of the day should include as much rest and pampering as time allows. You may want to get ready for the ceremony with the help of your wedding attendants or just your family or by yourself. If you are a person who is energized by being with people, you probably will want others around. If you get fatigued and need to restore your energy by being alone for a while, plan some rejuvenation time into the day's schedule.

Preparing Your Bodies for Your Wedding Night

You are going to share your bodies most intimately. To feel most relaxed and open with each other, it is important that your bodies are ready for this experience. If it will be the first time for either or both of you to have sexual intercourse, if it will be the first time for you to have sexual intercourse with each other, or if it will be the first time in a long time, you will want to make certain preparations to make the event go smoothly.

After many years of counseling couples about having a great wedding night, we have found several suggestions that we feel are critical. The following is our list of very specific tips—for the woman, the man, and for the couple together—to help you make your wedding night all it can be.

The Woman's Preparations

Get a recommendation for a gynecologist, medical practitioner, or nurse practitioner who is known to be thorough yet sensitive in examining and guiding women in preparing for marriage. Ask the examining clinician to inform you very specifically of the condition of your genitals and your readiness for sexual intercourse. You may ask about the condition of both your hymen and your vaginal muscle. If either seems tight, you may need to ask for graduated vaginal dilators. Never agree to surgery for relieving tightness unless that treatment is validated by at least two other clinicians. Surgery is rarely the best solution.

Be prepared to discuss contraceptive measures. If you plan to use a hormonal contraceptive, get started on the hormone of your choice at least two months before your wedding so your body has time to adjust. If you have complications or serious side effects, that will give you time to stop and start a hormone that interacts differently with your body.

Make sure you are clear of genital infections. Ask to be tested for AIDS, herpes simplex II, genital warts, and any other tests for sexually transmitted diseases your clinician would recommend. It would also be good to be sure you don't have a yeast infection. If the physician is willing, we would recommend getting a prescription for an antibiotic with a pain relieving medication to treat "honeymoon cystitis," should you get it. Honeymoon cystitis is an infection of the bladder that is common because of the sudden frequent sexual activity. Germs can easily travel into the urinary tract and cause a bladder infection that can be very painful. That pain is usually relieved relatively quickly after appropriate medications are taken.

In the months before your wedding night, get into the habit of tightening and relaxing your PC muscle, the muscle that controls the opening and closing of your vagina. Begin by identifying the sensation of tightening and relaxing this muscle. While sitting on the toilet to urinate, spread your legs apart. Start urination. Then stop urination for three seconds. Repeat this several times before you are finished emptying your bladder. If you have difficulty stopping urination, you need to work on tightening the PC muscle. If you have difficulty restarting urination, you need to work on voluntarily relaxing the PC muscle. If you can do both easily, you only need to tighten and relax the PC muscle twenty-five times per day to keep it in good condition.

Stretch the opening of your vagina every time you bathe or shower. Relaxing in warm water will help you relax your vaginal muscle so you can insert a dilator or your clean fingers. Begin with inserting one finger or a dilator the size of a tampon applicator. If you have difficulty inserting something that size, you can try a cotton-tipped applicator with a lubricant on it. Gradually increase the size of the object you insert to stretch the opening of your vagina until you are able to insert three fingers and stretch them apart. The circumference of an average erect penis is about four and a half to five and a half inches. When you insert the dilator, leave it in the vagina for about twenty minutes per day. The more faithful you are in preparing your vagina for entry, the more comfortable that initial experience will be. Since your vaginal muscle has either never been used for sexual intercourse before or it has been a long time since it has been used, you must think of preparing it for this special event as an athlete would prepare for an athletic event.

Groom your body especially carefully as the time for the wedding gets close. Different cultures and ethnic groups have standards of what is expected bodily preparation. In many Western cultures, the woman is expected to have smooth legs and underarms that have been freshly shaved, epilated, or waxed. The primary goal is for both you and your husband to feel good about your body.

The Man's Preparation

Just as the woman should make certain her body is healthy, free from infection, and ready for sexual intercourse, so should the man. It is wise to have a complete physical examination by a medical doctor. If you have any concerns related to your genitals, these can be dealt with at the time of your examination. The privacy of the physician's office is the place to address any questions. If your concerns or questions are minimized by the physician, that is a sign of the physician's inadequacy, not that you asked an inappropriate question. Find another doctor. Get tested for AIDS, genital warts, herpes simplex II, and any other sexually transmitted diseases that might be of concern. Testing for sexually transmitted diseases is a gift of trust you give each other. That is true whether or not you have been sexually active previously.

Whatever your practice of masturbation or your past sexual experience has been, you would do yourself and your new wife a big favor if you practiced, through self-stimulation, learning to extend ejaculation.

You can learn ejaculatory control by focusing on and savoring the pleasurable sensations, becoming aware of the warning signs that you are nearing ejaculation, stopping and starting stimulation, and/or squeezing the coronal ridge of the penis. Stimulation must be stopped or the squeeze applied long before you notice you are approaching the point of no return when you are about to ejaculate. Another important ingredient to learning to delay ejaculation is to rest or allow the intensity of the arousal to dissipate while you stop stimulation or apply the squeeze. Then resume stimulation. For more information refer to chapter 16 in our book *Restoring the Pleasure* or Helen Singer Kaplan's book *P.E.: Learning to Overcome Premature Ejaculation*.

Stimulating yourself to ejaculation within twenty-four hours before your wedding night will also be of great benefit to both you and your bride because on your wedding night you will likely be more excited and fatigued than usual and more apt to ejaculate quickly. This can be disappointing to both of you. A recent ejaculation will increase the time of pleasure and enjoyment for this first, memorable, married sexual experience.

Together Preparations

Take time to talk about and decide which contraceptive method the two of you would like to use. Decide which method has the most likelihood of success and is the most desirable for both of you. Once you have made your decision, obtain all of the necessary supplies you will need to effectively practice this method. Then familiarize yourselves with the process you have chosen.

If you will be using condoms, the man should practice applying the spermicide and the condom. If the diaphragm, cervical cap, sponge, or vaginal condom is your choice, the woman should practice inserting the device until it can be done with ease. If you are following a "natural" family-planning program, you both should be aware of where the woman will be in her cycle at the time of your wedding and honeymoon. Since the excitement surrounding the wedding can disrupt a woman's usual cycle, it might be wise to use an additional contraceptive for your wedding night and honeymoon. Or you might purchase and use an ovulation test kit. That would be an additional expense, but a worthwhile one.

Whatever your method of contraception, it is important that you are comfortable with it and can safely and efficiently use it so you avoid frustration—and pregnancy.

Once you have settled on your method of contraception, choose and purchase a lubricant. Since a woman lubricates vaginally early in a sexual experience, a time of long extended love play will require a lubricant. Whether or not you think you will need a lubricant, we recommend that all newly married couples automatically use one and that all couples have a lubricant available. Using a lubricant is not a sign of failure. Rather, to use a lubricant reduces demand and enhances pleasure because you do not have to pay attention to whether or when lubrication is occurring.

If you have chosen to use a rubber (latex) barrier contraceptive method, you should not use a lubricant that is oil- or petroleum-based. Oil and petroleum decrease the effectiveness of rubber (latex). Thus, you should not use Vaseline or other petroleum jellies, natural oils, mineral oil, butter, grease-based sexual lubricants, or some vaginal creams. These are unsafe to use with condoms, diaphragms, or cervical caps. You can use aloe, water, saliva, glycerin, and contraceptive foams, creams, and gels; commercial sexual lubricants include Probe, Astroglide, PrePair, Lubrin, Transi-Lube, Aqua-Lube, Condom-Mate, Duragel, and others; and water-based lubricants such as K-Y Jelly or Lubrafax. The water-based lubricants dry more quickly than others in the list, so they are not quite as desirable.

Allow for bodily preparation on the wedding night. If it has been a long time since you showered, shaved, and brushed your teeth, taking time to freshen your body for your time together may refresh you and increase your desirability to your spouse. The more carefully you have prepared your bodies for one another and the better prepared you are, the more positive your first sexual experience together will be. So take time to prepare carefully, and deliberately try to anticipate your every need and desire.

> *The more carefully you have prepared your bodies for one another and the better prepared you are, the more positive your first sexual experience together will be.*
>
> ❦ ❦

Having Sex for the First Time

It is not important whether you consummate your marriage (have your first married sexual intercourse) on the wedding night, the next day, or later during your honeymoon. It *is* important that you do not avoid each other. After a while, if you have not had sex and one of you is getting concerned about that, call time-out. Find out what is going on and how you might help.

Whenever you have sex for the first time after the wedding, *go slowly!* So many times, couples who have waited for marriage to have sexual intercourse are so eager (just as we were) that they bypass all the wonderful caressing, kissing, and fondling that were such a vital part of their physical interaction before. Now that they can do the "real thing," couples often forget about caressing, or they think the caressing and kissing are not necessary. But that is what made their bodies so hungry for the real thing; when they skip all that intense connecting, the sexual experience can be very quick and leave both feeling disappointed.

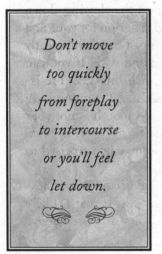

Don't move too quickly from foreplay to intercourse or you'll feel let down.

We recommend that you spend at least as much time enjoying the pleasure of each other's body as you would have on any date or time together before marriage. You might begin with your clothes on. As arousal and desire for more builds, gradually take off each other's clothes. Again, let the more hesitant one lead.

Generally this is where the man needs to slow down. We like how Paul Popenoe says it:

> Coming to the consummation of the marriage, few women will respond to "cave-man tactics" with anything but revulsion. Patience, self-control, and unselfishness on the part of the husband, always necessary, are never more important than during these first days and nights. A deter-

mination to place his own feelings second and to think first of the feelings of his wife, is the key to success.[2]

This reinforces the biblical teaching that the husband is to love his wife as Christ loved the church. That love is described this way in Philippians 2:3: "Do nothing out of selfish ambition or vain conceit, but in humility consider others better than yourselves."

For the woman, the way you can regard your husband as more important than yourself is to be an active participant. Just as your husband will need to focus more on the slowing-down part, you may need to attend to the second criterion for your first sexual experience: *Get active!* Your own frame of mind will greatly affect your first time together as husband and wife. If you can free yourself from all fears, false modesty, girlishness, and resistances, you will be able to listen to your body and communicate both verbally and physically what you would like. It is not your "duty" to please your husband; it is your "duty" to enjoy his body and go after your pleasure with gusto! You may be surprised to find that he is pleased by this enthusiasm.

Sometimes roles are reversed. It is the husband who is hesitant and fearful and the wife who is impatient. If that is likely to be the case for you, apply the opposite roles discussed above to your situation.

Connect with Each Other

We often recommend that married couples begin their sexual times by bathing and showering together. That is a way to relax, connect, and prepare your bodies for each other. In *Solomon on Sex*, Dillow refers to a Christian counselor friend, Don Meredith, who recommends this for the first night's experience:

> When they get to the motel, they are to draw a deep, relaxing bubble bath. Let the new bride get into the bath first while the husband is in the other room. A candle lit in the bathroom, being the only light, will produce a warm, romantic atmosphere. As they relax together in the bathtub,

they can discuss the day, talk, and even pray, thanking the
Lord for the gift of each other. As they communicate and
share, the warm water drains away the tensions of the day,
and the bubbles sufficiently hide the wife's body so she is
not immediately embarrassed.[3]

He goes on to recommend that they stimulate each other
under the water as a way of reducing inhibitions. If this idea
sounds good to both of you, try it.

You may not anticipate bathing together as a relaxing, connecting, and romantic event at all. Continue to talk about and
create your own first night. You may want to add a touch of surprise for each other, or you may not like any element of surprise,
even if it is romantic and meant to be positive. If you do not like
to be taken by surprise, let your fiancé know that immediately.

Pleasure Each Other

The only negative part of the bathtub scenario is that connection leads directly to stimulation. We would modify that
slightly by recommending playful genital touching under the water
and plenty of time before and/or after to really be passionate with
each other before pursuing direct, erotic stimulation. Touch, talk,
kiss, and explore every inch of one another's body to the degree
that you both feel free to do that. Soak in the good feelings of
being touched and touching. Have fun as you do. Nibble on each
other. Let each other know how much you enjoy the other. As you
enjoy yourselves, if anything you do is negative for the other, positively invite a different touch or activity. For example, if a touch is
too light and ticklish, ask for a heavier touch. Or if kissing gets too
intense or forceful, invite softer lips.

As you become ready for direct genital stimulation, invite
that by guiding your partner's hand to your genitals or rubbing
your genitals against your partner's body. Explore and learn
together what feels good. Do not expect that you will automatically know how to touch each other in the way that feels best.
Accept your spouse's guidance as a loving desire to enhance the

experience for both of you and a way to remove the demand for you to automatically know what feels right to him or her.

Allow the arousal to build in waves, enjoying the genital stimulation and then moving to other parts of the body. You want to keep each other hungry for more touch, not saturated so that you get irritated with the stimulation. This is particularly true for the man touching the woman. Direct clitoral stimulation is often more irritating than it is arousing. Most women prefer a flat hand over the clitoral area or fingers on either side of the clitoris to stroke the shaft rather than on the tip of the clitoris. Pain and pleasure are closely connected in the body, so if no pleasure is being stimulated you are furthest from triggering pain. The following graph illustrates how quickly direct stimulation can, with a slight shift in its intensity or location, change from causing peak arousal to instant pain. That is why it is so important for you, the woman, to signal your husband to let him know what you desire—because there is no other way he can know what you need and know when the stimulation gets too intense. You, the man, would do better to vary the stimulation automatically and keep your wife wanting more rather than pursuing orgasm too intensely. If you, as the woman, want to be stimulated to orgasm before entry and that is not a demand for performance but comes from the level of your arousal, go for it!

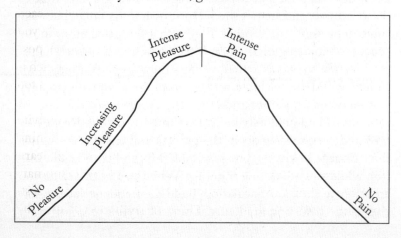

Entry should be attempted only at the woman's invitation. It is her body that is being entered; therefore, she should guide the penis into her vagina. When you, the woman, feel ready to allow entry, let your husband know that you desire him. It might be easiest for you to get on top of him while he is on his back. He or you can apply lubricant to his penis and separate your labia (lips) and apply lubricant to the opening of your vagina. Use his penis as a paintbrush over the opening of your vagina and on your clitoris. Poke the penis into your vagina just a little. Tighten and relax your PC muscle as you do. Intentionally relax your vaginal muscle as you guide his penis in. You may need to push against his penis to push through your hymen and vaginal muscle.

If you experience resistance, it is usually because the labia are stuck together, you're pushing at the wrong place (that is, you are not quite at the opening or do not have the penis at quite the right angle to enter the vagina), your hymen is a little tough to break, or your vaginal muscle is not relaxed. The latter is the most likely. Remember you are both new at this; just enjoy the process of trying. Play around with different positions if one doesn't work. Stretch or dilate the vagina and try again. Get a hand mirror and together try to figure out what is happening. Do not keep trying until you are frustrated. Stop while the attempts are fun, get some sleep, and pursue pleasure again when you have time to do so leisurely and are not tired. Don't rush to try entry, but continue to pleasure one another. Play with attempts at entry in the process of enjoying each other. If frustration ensues, seek help.

When the penis actually enters the vagina, you may want to stop, withdraw, celebrate, and try entry again later. Or you may just lie quietly together and enjoy the closeness of this special moment. Then gradually build rhythmic thrusting. Rest every now and then to slow down the process and enjoy every sensation. Engage in kissing, breast stimulation, and clitoral stimulation while you are resting together. When you both decide you are ready to thrust to ejaculation, build the frequency and intensity of the thrusting gradually. Think of trying to enjoy every moment and make it last as long as possible, like licking your favorite ice-cream cone. Resist the urge to thrust or to pursue ejaculation too quickly. That will end your time quickly and may be disappointing. If that should happen by mistake, don't get down on yourselves. You have years to learn to extend intercourse. You may have some regrets about this first time, but if your expectations were realistic you know that is normal. Savor the good feelings of being together and stay connected. If you, the woman, need more stimulation, ask for that. The husband can also offer that.

Spend time talking and cuddling when you finish. Affirm each other. Let each other know what you enjoyed. Share fantasies of other possibilities for sexual play if those ideas don't intimidate. Have tissue, washcloths, a small towel, or some type of wipes at the bedside to catch the seminal fluid and vaginal secretions after sex. There will be a bit of a mess, but the woman can easily handle that by putting tissue or a washcloth between her legs to catch the secretions as they seep out of her vagina. The man can wipe off his penis as necessary.

It would be quite common, if this is your first sexual experience and you have not been bringing yourselves or each other to orgasm, for the woman not to be orgasmic. When we got married, we didn't really even understand about orgasm, so Joyce probably wasn't orgasmic at first, but it wasn't an issue for us. We don't even know whether she was or wasn't. We both loved our times together and remember them, including the wedding night, with great fondness. Now those initial experiences would seem disappointing for us, but they were not disappointing then! And this is appropriate. Our lack of unrealistic TV and movie-star models and our naiveté prevented us from having any pressure-producing goals. That was a perfect start for our sexual life together. You, too, need not be disappointed if the orgasmic reflex doesn't happen for you initially. If you are allowing arousal, enjoy that and let it build and extend. Eventually, the reflex of orgasm is likely to get triggered, especially if you are active and uninhibited. If you feel frustrated or feel like crying because you have not had release, recognize that as one way your body may be letting down and releasing the tension buildup of the sexual arousal in your body. Hold each other and share the crying. Do not take it as a sign of failure and avoid each other. Bring that release into your connected feelings.

Your first sexual experience will be enhanced if your spouse is a sensitive, informed partner who is willing to talk about feelings; if it occurs in a safe location and is not rushed; if you use adequate birth control and protection against sexually transmitted diseases (if either of you is a potential carrier); and if you are ready emotionally to risk that level of intimacy and vulnerability.

Common Questions and Their Answers

Preparing for your first married sex is a topic that has elicited numerous questions from the premarital couples we have taught. Here, we will attempt to answer the most commonly asked questions on this topic.

1. Do most women experience bleeding and pain when the hymen breaks during the first entry?

The response can range from absolutely no pain and no bleeding to such severe pain that entry is impossible and there is noticeable bleeding. The last two possibilities are rare. When the vaginal opening has been stretched and a lubricant is used, and when the woman guides the penis in at her own pace, there is often no bleeding and only a momentary "Ouch!"

2. What can I do to reduce my fear of the pain of intercourse? I am a virgin and I am dreading the wedding night. I have always avoided pain at any cost.

Unfortunately, your *fear* is likely to cause pain unless you work past it. The fear will not go away by ignoring it. Talk about it, and prepare, prepare, prepare! Stretch your vaginal opening at least twenty minutes daily. Get a gynecological examination, and ask your physician for dilators. Learn to control your PC muscle so you can voluntarily relax it. Learn visualization and relaxation techniques. Every day when you stretch your vagina, picture your first sexual intercourse. Note when your fear sets in. Replace the fear with positive thoughts and feelings. Imagine the penis in your vagina feeling like a warm, soft, moist, loving sensation. Take charge of when and how entry happens. Use lots of lubricant. Let your husband know as soon as you feel afraid. Stop pursuing entry at that point and just hold and affirm one another, then try again. Often anticipation is the biggest hurdle. Once you actually pursue entry, the fears may dissipate. If you cannot get beyond your fear, get help from a sexual therapist.

3. Does the woman's expanding her vagina before intercourse take away from God's plan for the woman to be a virgin?

No. A virgin is a woman who has not had sexual intercourse. She has not had a penis in her vagina. She has not "become one" with a man. She is still a virgin!

4. What can I do to relax the muscle during intercourse so that my vagina isn't so tight?

Practice the PC muscle exercises described on page 82— so you can control that muscle when you choose to relax it. Learn total-body relaxation techniques. When you notice the vaginal muscle is tight, try bearing down like you do when you are having a bowel movement, but now you are pretending you are pushing something out of your vagina.

5. What if my wife is initially aroused and then loses lubrication before entry?

This is very common. That is why we recommend using a lubricant every time until you notice you have forgotten to use it. Lubrication occurs within ten to twenty seconds of any genital stimulation. During prolonged love play, lubrication is likely to dry.

6. What techniques can be used to tell the other person that what they are doing is pleasurable?

Nonverbal or verbal responsiveness is a strong reinforcer and very contagious. You can moan, groan, or let your spouse know that right at this moment you feel like you could do what you're doing forever.

7. How does a woman stimulate a man so he is prepared for entry by her invitation?

The woman's invitation for entry should not be a demand that the man must be ready at that moment. It just means that whenever he is ready, she is. Often, if the woman is ready, her arousal will have gotten the man eager too. The woman participates in preparing the man for entry, not only by her own involvement and responsiveness, but also by enjoying her husband's genitals. Stroking the shaft of the penis, in addition to enjoying his entire body, will usually get a man ready for entry.

8. Is "quiet vagina" for newly marrieds only?

No. Quiet vagina (resting without thrusting after entry) is used by couples throughout their married lives as a means to extend sexual pleasure after entry and to delay ejaculation for men.

9. Isn't it uncomfortable for the woman to lead?

It depends so much on how she leads. If she is controlling, demeaning, or demanding, it is very uncomfortable. If she sets the pace by being open about what she is feeling and desiring and her husband sensitively responds to her, it can be wonderful for both. The woman is more variable and complex in her need for emotional readiness, in her physical responsiveness, and in her sexual desires than the man is. Because of this, it usually works best if the man delights in the woman but lets her set the pace, as Solomon did in the Old Testament.

If a woman is experienced and her husband is not, it will be very important for her to lead until they are equally comfortable with the sexual activity.

10. Must a woman have an orgasm every time?

Some women feel a need for an orgasm every time; others do not. There is no right or wrong. The woman's enjoyment of the sexual experience may have nothing to do with having an orgasm. For her it may be the closeness and connection that is most satisfying. This varies greatly from woman to woman. A successful sexual experience is not dependent upon arousal, orgasm, ejaculation, or intercourse.

11. It seems like after waiting so long for sex, we're going to want to go right to sexual intercourse on our wedding night. Is it detrimental to go right from foreplay to intercourse without getting acquainted with each other's genitals?

Getting acquainted with each other's genitals, even though it seems like that would be beneficial to do before pursuing sexual intercourse, is likely to feel rather clinical and exposing for a newly married couple. Even couples who have been married for years sometimes have difficulty being that vulnerable with each other. We don't think that would be a necessary step to consummating your marriage. It is natural on the wedding night to just let down all restrictions and go for it. Do be sure to include the conditions described previously for a "successful" wedding-night experience so you don't move too quickly from foreplay to intercourse and feel let down.

12. What if the man wants sex two to three times per day? Should the woman submit?

It is interesting that the question states, "the man wants sex," not that he desires his wife. Usually the man who wants sex that often is not responding to an urge that is growing out of his closeness and enjoyment of his wife. Rather, he is an insecure person who is using sex to get affirmation. This will kill the woman's sexual desire by the end of the honeymoon, if not sooner. So our answer to the question would be: not if he wants to enjoy an involved sexual partner for the rest of his life!

13. How do you avoid getting into a sexual rut?

You probably don't have to worry about that quite yet, but it's wise to be aware of that possibility. Joyce had been taught in her premarital class before our wedding that a couple should not get into a sexual rut. Being a good student, she thought we had to try a new position every time we had sex on our honeymoon, when we had not even mastered the basics!

The best way not to get into a rut is to allow quality time for your sex life and to learn to guide each other in the sexual experience. If each of you takes the responsibility to listen to each other's needs and desires and communicate them to one another without demand, you won't have to keep trying to figure out what works and then keep doing over and over what worked once. Rote repetition of what worked once is a sure way to get into a rut and diminish the spark of your sexual relationship.

14. How do we cope with "morning breath" without breaking spontaneity by jumping out of bed to brush our teeth?

Couples are affected differently by nighttime or morning breath. Some are not bothered at all; it's just not an issue for them. In the most challenging situation, one spouse is extremely sensitive to breath and the other is not. That can cause conflict because the insensitive one feels criticized by the sensitive one, and the sensitive one feels disregarded by the insensitive one. Whether one or both spouses are aware of bad-breath issues, they can work out a plan that easily takes care of stale breath: keep breath mints or breath spray at the bedside.

15. How important is it for both of us to have clean hands and bodies to protect the other from developing irritations or infections?

It is very important to be clean. Nails should be filed and smooth, hands should be freshly washed, teeth should be brushed and flossed, and genitals should be clean. The hands and genitals are especially important—the hands because they fondle the genital openings, which are a clean part of the body that become infected when exposed to germs, and the genitals because they can easily become contaminated by feces from the rectum. When freshly washed and free of infection, the genitals are clean.

16. Are you at risk for contracting an STD if you have never had sexual intercourse?

If neither you nor your spouse have had genital-to-genital, oral-to-genital, or genital-to-anal contact, you are not at risk of contracting most STDs. Sometimes an individual who has not been sexually active can carry the virus that causes genital warts. It may remain dormant for years and become activated during sexual intercourse. Authorities are not certain how the person's body acquired the virus in the first place. It might have been through sharing used swimming suits or public swimming pools. The oral herpes simplex I virus may have been transferred to the genitals through oral-genital stimulation. We recommend that you both be tested for STDs whether or not you have engaged in behaviors that transmit them. It will take care of any doubts and build trust that the two of you are starting clean with each other.

17. If I was tested for AIDS six months after my last sexual contact, do I need to be tested again?

Yes, you do. The virus causing AIDS may not show up on a blood test until after six months, so you need to keep getting tested every six months until the wedding. Usually you will be considered safe after a year, but new information is continually being made available on the reliability of AIDS testing, so call an AIDS testing service for the current information.

18. How do I deal with the memories of past sexual partners, positive and negative? How can I rid myself of the guilt connected with these past experiences? What can I (or we) do now to minimize the negative effects my past may have on our marriage?

This is a difficult, yet common, struggle for many couples entering marriage today. We believe Scripture's teaching that sex is for marriage, because it was designed to prevent this very dilemma. The conditions of married sex are different than sex outside of a committed relationship. That sex is often associated with risk, guilt, winning, keeping, conquering, rebelling, and/or deceiving. If your previous sex was connected with any of these conditions, you will need to "undo" that past so it won't negatively affect your sex life in your marriage. Memories of past sexual partners easily move into the marriage bed with you. They may show up in your marriage as comparisons, self-doubt, distrust, dissatisfaction, or fear.

First, you need to deal with your guilt. God's grace is adequate to forgive and erase any past sins. Confession is often as much for one's peace of mind as it is for one's relationship with God. You may want to take some time to pray with someone about your past. It may be helpful to write out all the incidents that haunt your memory and need to be cleansed. Then ask God to erase them for you. Keep bringing them to him until you are freed of their presence in your life.

Second, how you deal with your fiancé is important. It is important to tell him or her that your past still affects you and that you want to be free of it and get it out of the way of your current relationship. Do not share details of that past; otherwise the memories will also haunt your fiancé. Share how it affects you, what you have done about it, and how you would like to work together to minimize or eliminate its effects on your marriage.

Listen to, reflect, and care about your fiancé's feelings about your past. It will be easy for you to get defensive if his or her reaction is one of hurt, anger, or distrust. The more you understand that your fiancé's reactions are most natural, and the more you allow for them, the sooner they will decrease.

Third, together make a plan for dealing with this past within your marriage. Start as if your married sexual relationship is the first experience for both of you. Learn about each other as unique sexual beings totally different from those past partners. Do not start sexually at the place you left off. Start as a new learner. Let your spouse teach you about himself or herself. When that past sneaks in, have a plan to signal each other and distract each other from those thoughts, feelings, or comparisons and focus more diligently on each other. Continually affirm your love and commitment to each other by your words and your actions. You will need to be more deliberate about this than someone without past sexual partners.

19. Because we are considered "new" through Christ, can we let go of past experiences and look at our wedding night as a first experience?

Yes and no. In God's eyes—and spiritually inside yourselves—you can reclaim your virginity, and your wedding night will be your first sexual experience. Emotionally and physically, however, you must deal realistically with your past experiences and how they will impact your wedding night.

20. We have decided to wait for marriage to consummate our sexual relationship. That used to be a struggle for us, but it no longer is. Could we have shut off our feelings for each other?

It certainly sounds like that may be what happened. When we teach premarital classes, we always caution that if a premarital couple has decided not to be sexually active before marriage and that is not a struggle for them, they better get some help. God has designed us to desire sexual intimacy with the person we love and commit ourselves to. That is our responsiveness. We are given the responsibility to manage that drive so we do not violate ourselves, our partner, or our relationship with God. Therefore, sexual activity should be controlled by the decisions we make and the conditions we put ourselves into, not by turning off our desire for that intimacy.

Since the two of you seem to have already turned off your "pilot lights," it is time to relight those desires. Saying "I do" will not turn the switch back on. Between now and your wedding, reengage in times of passionate kissing that go no further than that. If you sense an urge for more, affirm those good feelings by telling each other about them, but stick to just kissing. As desire builds, allow yourselves more bodily contact, but always after deciding upon very clear behavioral boundaries. Don't allow your actions to go further than what you have decided upon, but allow your desire for more to build. Don't ever stop those natural urges, but control the level of your sexual involvement by the settings you allow yourselves to be in and the physical behaviors you allow yourselves to engage in.

21. While we are going to wait until we get married before having sex, what sexual activities are permissible until that time?

We use the Bible as our standard, and it offers no direct answer as to what sexual activity other than intercourse is not permissible outside of marriage. Therefore, we apply to this specific question the Bible's consistent message that sex is for marriage. And marriage throughout Scripture is clearly identified as a monogamous, heterosexual relationship characterized by fidelity. Therefore, we look at how the activity a couple engages in *before* marriage is likely to affect their sexual life *after* marriage.

What we find most positively affects sex in marriage is keeping sexual feelings and desires alive before marriage while engaging only in sexual activities that do not violate either of you, your relationship with each other, or your relationship with God. Thus, you should not practice any sexual behavior that is associated with risk or guilt. You should not be doing any sexual act to keep your husband-to-be. Sexual acts should not be connected with rebellion, drugs, or alcohol, or any other conditions that will tarnish sex after marriage. Remember that 1 Thessalonians 4 teaches that one who abstains from sexual immorality knows "how to possess his own vessel" and does not "transgress and defraud" another person sexually.

Choose together what your sexual boundaries will be, how you will keep to those decisions, and what action you will take if your boundaries are violated. Before marriage, keep sexual desires and feelings alive while making conscious, active choices about your behavior. This will best prepare you for a life of marital sexual fulfillment.[4]

7

Getting Married When Your Parents Don't Approve

❧ John Trent ❧

It should have been one of the most wonderful times of her life. Stacy grew up in a loving Christian home, with parents who had encouraged and blessed her since she was born. Now, in her senior year of college, Stacy had met the man she was sure God wanted her to marry.

He may not have been the cutest date she'd ever brought home. But he certainly had the highest standards and character, and the best family background. Stacy hadn't laughed as much, felt so free to share her deepest heart feelings and dreams, nor fell so deeply in love with anyone before.

The young man of Stacy's dreams was headed into ministry, not marketing like her last serious boyfriend. To her it was inconceivable her parents would frown on someone who made her feel so full of light and life. But the unthinkable did happen.

One night, Stacy told her mother, "I think David is going to ask me to marry him . . . and I hope he does. I love him with all my heart, Mom."

Stacy had expected fireworks to go off when she shared her heart. Only she thought they'd be outbursts of celebration, not condemnation. For the next hour, she sat through emotional salvo after salvo that ripped holes into her choice for a mate, her lifelong dreams, and to a degree, her relationship with her parents. Her mother had a myriad of reasons why David wasn't right. According to her, David didn't seem to be smart enough or mature enough. "To be honest," her mother confided, "I'm not sure you'd like being a minister's wife."

Stacy had always had a good relationship with her parents. Now she felt trapped between hurting the man she loved, and her mother who was like a best friend. After that first traumatic night, it seemed that every conversation came around to David, and every mention of his name spawned a heated argument between them. To top it off, her father's "neutral" stand made her feel angry and confused by his seeming indifference.

Stacy had always dreamed of filling her room with bridal magazines, sharing memories with her mother, and crying with joy. Now she was crying all right. Only it was alone in her room, feeling like an eight-year-old who was considered incapable of making a major decision. The tears she shed were from damaging words on both sides that she knew she'd never forget. For the first time in her life, she seriously considered eloping . . . but would that be right?

Sound familiar?

It does to me.

In fact, it's a familiar scenario to most of us who work with premarital couples across the country.

For almost twenty years I've had the privilege of teaching and counseling couples and families. Some fifteen years ago, I designed and began to teach a mandatory eight-week premarital program at our home church that still is offered every spring and fall. To date, well over a thousand couples have completed the course, and I've heard dozens, if not fully a hundred stories like Stacy's. In each case, the details are unique, but the problem is the same:

"What do I do when my parents don't approve of our marriage?"

Waking Up a Wolverine

I have to admit it. When I was asked to write on this subject, I felt like I was the one being asked to take a short stick and wake up a sleeping wolverine. That's because there's no way you can talk about a subject so emotional, so laden with long-term potential hurt for both parents and grown children, without offending someone. Yet before you start growling, let's look together at several of the biblical issues behind this challenging situation.

First, we'll take a look at an important question. Namely, "I know I need to 'honor' my parents . . . but is that the same as obeying them?" Then, we'll take a look at the deep need we all have for our parents to accept our person, our decisions, and our potential spouse. In short, why is it so important that we get their "blessing"?

After talking about this deep need, I'll give you a short test. Your score will take you down either one of two paths. Each path will explore several key aspects and feelings of both adult children and their parents. Then we'll wrap up our discussion with a clear challenge for you to evaluate what you've learned and plan your next step.

If I've done my job well, then I'll have put you within a "three-foot circle" of making your own decision. In golf language, that's getting the ball close enough to the hole (within a three-foot circle) that you can tap it in with your next stroke.

In other words, my goal in this chapter isn't to make a decision for you. Only you can do that. Facing a parent's disapproval of a marriage may be one of the most difficult things you've ever experienced. *It's tremendously difficult.* And if you don't think so,

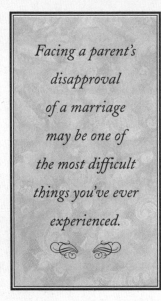

Facing a parent's disapproval of a marriage may be one of the most difficult things you've ever experienced.

then you're not thinking clearly about the potential lifelong hurt that can result!

That's why it's important that you think long and hard about this incredibly complicated emotional and spiritual area. When you finish this chapter, it's my prayer you'll have carefully considered several key factors before making any decision. And then, in God's timing, as you do make your decision to step forward—mark time —or step away—you'll feel wholeheartedly that's what God would have you do.

So, to begin, let's look at a biblical basic. Namely, we all know (or should know) that one of God's clear commandments is to "Honor your father and your mother" (Exodus 20:12). In fact, it's not only one of the great Ten Commandments, but it's the first commandment that has a promise linked to it: "That you may live long in the land the LORD your God is giving you."

That's a serious promise! Honor your parents, or you won't live long! But is "honor" the same as "obedience"?

Obedience and Honor

In the story that began this chapter, one of the things Stacy's mother was quick to say to her was, "You're still our child. We're telling you, this young man is not right for you, and you need to obey what we say. Period."

Can you see her mother's logic, and if followed, the inescapable position this puts Stacy in? Since she is their child, and since children are to obey their parents (see Ephesians 6:1 if you've still got a question about that), Stacy's only choice is to obey her mother—or go against both her and God.

It's absolutely true that children should obey. But what happens when, like Stacy, that "child" is a fourth-year college student who pays rent at home and is responsible for all her finances at school? Is she an adult, fully independent and able to make a decision apart from her parents? Or because she's still living at home, is she still technically a child who needs to obey ... period?

First of all, during biblical times, you didn't see the kind of extended adolescence we have in our day and age. In fact, there was a clear line between being a child and being an adult. When a young man or woman came of age, there was a celebration attended by family, community, and friends—still echoed today in the Jewish "bar mitzvah" and "bat mitzvah." Even Paul noted this line between being a *pideon*—Greek for a small child—and an adult, saying, "When I was a child *[pideon]*, I talked like a child, I thought like a child, I reasoned like a child. When I became a man, I put childish ways behind me" (1 Corinthians 13:11).

Obedience to parents is something asked of children in Ephesians. Yet each one of us is commanded to give honor to our parents—that's something we never outgrow.

The word *honor* in Scripture means something is "heavy, weighty," like gold. What does its opposite, *dishonor*, literally mean? "Mist" or "steam." Do you get the picture?

When we honor people, we treat them like they're heavyweights. That means we respect their opinions. We grant them a weighty place in our lives, and we seek to uplift their names and persons. Dishonoring them means treating what they say or do as carrying as little weight as steam. It means looking at them (or their words) as an annoying mist to be wiped away, like a steamy mirror after a shower.

In short, as adults, we're called to give great weight and honor to our parents. We're to highly value them and what they have to say—even about the person and timing of our wedding. If we're still living under their roof, and are sustained by their finances, then we may well be obligated to obey their counsel—even if we're past legal adult age. However, if we are an adult, with independent means and responsibilities, then our primary obedience is to our heavenly Father and his revealed Word. Biblically, as independent adults, what we owe our parents is honor, not unquestioned obedience.

In our example of Stacy, she was fully responsible for her expenses, and she was a legal adult. Before everything blew up, she already had her parents' blessing to move out of the house and into an apartment with a Christian roommate. And because she was moving away from home, she'd already saved and lined up a health-care policy of her own.

After she moved out, you could certainly say she was free as an adult to make the decision she felt most honored the Lord. Actually, both Stacy and her fiancé had strong grounds to make an independent decision and move forward with the wedding.

As adults, we transfer our primary obedience from our parents to the Word of God. For example, if your parents are objecting to your impending marriage because you're a Christian and your fiancé isn't, they have biblical grounds for their opposition. (See 2 Corinthians 6:14 if you have questions about that issue.) If your marriage in some way directly confronts a biblical truth, then it's God you're struggling with, not just your parents.

But in Stacy's case, they were both growing Christians. Yet while she may have had the biblical right to go against her parents' wishes, she still agonized over something she wanted more than being right. She wanted her parents' blessing. I'm convinced almost everyone I've met does too.

What is this blessing, and why is it so important to those getting married?

Why a Parental Blessing Is Important

I'm convinced that one of the deepest needs we have as humans is to receive our parents' blessing. Just listen to these words of deep anguish spoken by a son who never got his father's blessing.

> When Esau heard his father's words, he burst out with a loud and bitter cry and said to his father, "Bless me—me too, my father!" (Genesis 27:34)

I was finishing my doctoral program and working at a psychiatric hospital when I made a life-changing discovery. At the same time I was busy completing my school program, I was also teaching a study on the book of Genesis at our home church.

While I'd read the story of Jacob and Esau a hundred times before, that night, as I read the story of these twin brothers, suddenly a light went on. Here were two brothers, searching for, even willing to steal to get the same thing—a blessing from their father.

I'm convinced that one of the deepest needs we have as humans is to receive our parents' blessing.

I knew from my Old Testament studies that Esau's pain-wrapped cry didn't come from getting cut out of the will, or losing property rights. Esau had already *sold* his inheritance to his brother Jacob for a simple pot of stew. But now, when it comes to his father's blessing, Esau falls apart. When he finds out he will never receive a blessing, he cries out a second time, saying:

> "Do you have only one blessing, my father? Bless me too, my father!" (Genesis 27:38)

As I sat at my desk that night, I was suddenly stunned by what I'd read. I realized I was hearing Esau's words repeated every day at the psychiatric hospital I worked at. In a hundred different ways, I would hear a man or woman say, "Please, Mom, give me your blessing" or, "Please, Dad, I need your blessing. *Mom, Dad . . . why didn't you bless me!*"

Then I thought of my own background, and growing up in a single-parent home. Fully a thousand times I myself had wanted my father's blessing, even though I never saw him when I was growing up, and only saw him rarely as an adult.

That night, I began an in-depth study of what lay behind Esau's painful cry—the biblical concept of the "blessing." It became the subject of my doctoral dissertation. And when I teamed up with Gary Smalley several years ago, we took the work from my dissertation and turned it into an entire book on the subject (*The Gift of the Blessing*, Thomas Nelson, 1993).

In my study of Scripture, I discovered many different types of blessings. For example, if you were going to go on a long trip (which in Old Testament times meant going beyond the horizon), you'd have a blessing put on you that asked for God's protection. A priest could give a blessing to an entire congregation (like Aaron's words, "May the Lord bless and keep you and make his face to shine upon you"). And yes, there were blessings given to those getting married (like for both Isaac and Jacob's marriages).

Whenever there was a major turning point in a person's life—a move, a marriage, the birth of a child, last words—these were times when blessings were given, or withheld. And while there were many occasions when blessings were given, there were several specific elements that never change. In fact, whether it was a priest, parent, grandparent, or Jesus himself blessing children, you see five consistent elements that were always present.

Let's briefly look at these five elements, for in them, I think you'll see why and what makes a parental blessing so desired and important. (The very thing that made Stacy and her fiancé delay their wedding for a time.) Then, you'll be given a short test that will lead you down one of two paths.

A Closer Look at the Blessing

In the Scriptures, the word *blessing* literally means "to bow the knee." It's a word that came from a camel bending its knees so its rider could climb up on its back. Falling on our knees before someone very valuable is what the word came to mean. That's why, for instance, the psalmist writes so powerfully, "Bless the LORD, O my soul" (Psalm 103:1 KJV). In other words, "Lord, you're so worthy of praise and honor, I fall before you!"

Now obviously, the blessing parents gave their children wasn't to literally fall on their knees before their children! But there were always at least five elements present when they blessed them. As I go through each one, make a mental checklist to see if you received one, two, three, four, or perhaps all five of these elements as you were growing up.

1. Appropriate, Meaningful Touch

Always when the blessing was given in the Scriptures, you'd see appropriate, meaningful touch. Jacob's father, Isaac, says to his son, "Come here, my son, and kiss me" (Genesis 27:26). The "laying on of hands," a hug, a kiss, or some form of appropriate touch was a key element of the blessing. When Jesus blessed the children, we're told he took them in his arms and blessed them.

Did you grow up in a home where there was appropriate, meaningful touch? (Remember, Jacob was at least forty years old when his father told him to give him a hug and a kiss!)

2. Spoken Messages

A blessing was always audibly spoken. I've counseled with hundreds of people over the years who have told me they "knew" they were loved—but they never *heard* the words. Yet like a fill-in-the-blank test with the right word waiting to be filled in, not hearing verbally that we're loved and special can leave an empty space in our heart. (Remember Stacy's anguish over her father's silence regarding her marriage?)

Did you grow up hearing, orally, that you were loved and valuable?

3. Attaching High Value

Remember the literal meaning behind the blessing. It was to "bow the knee." In our culture, we don't bow before others as people do in many Eastern countries. In fact, during the

Olympics, the American flag has never dipped before foreign royalty in the parade of nations.

Attaching high value to others doesn't have to involve literally bowing before them, but it does communicate clearly—like with appropriate touch and spoken words—that this person is of high value.

Did you grow up feeling like you had high value to your parents? More than the television or their careers? Do you feel that way today?

4. Special Future

One key aspect of the blessing in the Scriptures was how it was always a special time to ask for God's blessing on that person's future. Children tend to be literalists when it comes to what they hear about their future from their parents. Children who grow up with the blessing hear things like, "You can be all God designed you to be." "You're so sensitive (or wise or honest or caring or hardworking), I wouldn't be surprised if God uses that trait in a mighty way in the future."

Children who miss out on this element of the blessing are those who hear things like, "Don't take algebra—that's for the smart kids!" or "Don't think a fat mess like you is going to get a date with anyone decent."

If we've never heard from our parents that we have a special future, we will have a hard time believing it's true—but it is. Jeremiah 29:11 tells us, "'For I know the plans I have for you,' declares the LORD, 'plans to prosper you and not to harm you, plans to give you hope and a future.'"

Did you grow up hearing and believing your parents felt you had a special future in store for you? Did they ask God's blessing on your future?

5. Genuine Commitment

This final aspect of the blessing is what makes it more than just words or a quick hug. When the blessing was given in the

Scriptures, it involved parents making a full commitment of their words and selves. It meant that they were there for you emotionally, spiritually, and physically.

Those five elements—appropriate, meaningful touch, spoken messages, attaching high value, special future, and genuine commitment—form the backbone of the parental blessings in the Scriptures.

Now armed with that insight, ask yourself this question. "Would you like those five things from your parents as you get married?"

A Parent's Blessing

Would you like to see their eyes light up when they see you and your fiancé together? Could you picture being met with a warm handshake, hug, or appropriate kiss on the cheek when you get together?

Would you like to hear words of praise for you and your loved one? Words that acknowledged their parental pride in who you've become in the Lord and gratefulness for the person he's brought you?

How would it feel to know that they highly valued your choice of a life partner and thought well of your decision-making process?

Wouldn't it be nice to hear wishes or even predictions for a God-blessed special future for you two, and if God wills, a future family?

Do you desire their genuine commitment to love both you and your life partner, through thick and thin?

If these five elements reflect what you want to see, hear, and feel from your parents, it's safe to say you're looking for their blessing. But here's an important question. The answer to this question will take you down one of two different paths: "As their child growing up, did you already receive their blessing—or is it something you're still waiting for?"

Politically Correct Praise

In our culture, a wedding is perhaps the most significant event where giving a blessing is socially acceptable. Even parents who may not have spoken loving words for years often burst forth with sentimentality or even genuine words of praise at a wedding.

I remember my wedding to Cindy some eighteen years ago. Cindy's father doesn't know the Lord, and is a rough construction worker who is slow to speak affirming words. But after the rehearsal dinner, as we stood in the parking lot, he quickly hugged my wife. He mumbled a rare, "I love you," said he was proud of her (his only daughter), and was glad I'd be a part of their family. Then, almost as an afterthought, he said to me, "Remember . . . if you don't want her, we'll take her back!"

Sure, his blessing won't end up on a Hallmark card. It might even seem like a backhanded slap at me! (Which it wasn't.) But Cindy saw what happened in that parking lot for what it was. Meaningful touch. Spoken words of love. High value. His best attempt at giving her his blessing before the wedding.

Her father's words weren't eloquent, but they were still important for Cindy. It's important for *any* of us to have our parents' blessing. Yet for many people (like Esau), years of waiting for words of blessing catapults the expectation level into the stratosphere.

I've talked with many people who, as adults, with the wedding looming, are almost desperate to have their parents' blessing. It's as if a blessing at that strategic time somehow helps close the loop on their childhood and provides a boost of confidence for their future.

Did you receive your parents' blessing growing up? Do you have it now? To help answer those questions, stop now and take a short test. Your total score will direct you to which path to take next.

Did You Receive the Blessing?

Circle your response to each element of the blessing. (Even if your parents divorced, like mine did, circle your response. Feel free to consider a stepparent if your parents remarried.)

Appropriate Meaningful Touch

from my mother

1   2   3   4   5   6   7

Rarely received it   Consistently received it

from my father

1   2   3   4   5   6   7

Rarely received it   Consistently received it

Spoken Message

from my mother

1   2   3   4   5   6   7

Rarely received it   Consistently received it

from my father

1   2   3   4   5   6   7

Rarely received it   Consistently received it

Attaching High Value

from my mother

1   2   3   4   5   6   7

Rarely received it   Consistently received it

from my father

1   2   3   4   5   6   7

Rarely received it   Consistently received it

Special Future

from my mother

1   2   3   4   5   6   7

Rarely received it   Consistently received it

from my father

1   2   3   4   5   6   7

Rarely received it   Consistently received it

Genuine Commitment

from my mother

1	2	3	4	5	6	7

Rarely received it   Consistently received it

from my father

1	2	3	4	5	6	7

Rarely received it   Consistently received it

1 ———————————— 15 ———————————— 35

Total Score

Place an "0" on the line for your mother's total score, and a "X" on the line for your father's total score. For example:

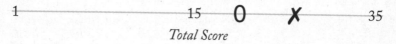

1 ———————————— 15   **0**   **X**   35

Total Score

Now, total your score for your mother first, and then your father. A high score (24 and up) indicates a high degree of warmth and expressed affirmation from your parents growing up. Scores in midrange are common, and lower scores (in the low teens or single digits) often indicate either an absent, passive, or difficult parental situation.

Now that you've scored how you've done in experiencing your parents' blessing in the past, use your total score to head down one of two paths. If you're confident you received your parents' blessing, read this next section titled, "Path One: If You Received Your Parents' Blessing." If you're confident you didn't receive it, then either keep reading, or skip forward to the section titled, "Path Two: If You Did Not Receive Your Parents' Blessing." For some of you, it's a judgment call either way. Feel free to read both sections that follow.

Path One: If You Received Your Parents' Blessing

When I counsel premarital couples who are struggling with their parents' lack of acceptance of their wedding, I always bring up the blessing we've just talked about. For those who have consistently received their parents' love, encouragement, and affirmation in the past (like Stacy's situation shared earlier), meeting resistance from a parent can be particularly disconcerting. Here are several things to consider if you're confident of your parents' love and acceptance of you as a person.

Are your parents merely being protective and possessive?

The Song of Songs is God's picture of an ideal courtship and marriage. Listen to this strong expression of love: "Place me like a seal over your heart, like a seal on your arm; for love is as strong as death, its jealousy unyielding as the grave" (Song of Songs 8:6).

Don't think that possessiveness is an immature aspect of love. The Lord himself says of his people, "But the LORD has taken you, and brought you forth out of the iron furnace, out of Egypt, to be a people of his own possession" (Deuteronomy 4:20 RSV). Genuine love is possessive.

If you know your parents love you deeply, perhaps they're struggling with letting go, with entrusting you—their priceless gift from God—to a stranger. The best antidote in this case is time. If you met your fiancé on a Tuesday, and now it's Saturday and you're engaged, expect their loving response to be one of possessive protection. Often, an engagement period of six months to a year is enough to help a parent make the transition from protective fright to warm acceptance.

What is the character of your future spouse?

Consider another principle: A godly character is crucial in the person you're to marry. Is that the case? Or are there some major blemishes in your loved one's life that you've accepted or explained away, and yet your parents see them apart from any emotional attachment or clouding.

In Bible times, one common way to purify oil was to pour the unrefined olive oil through a series of trays, stacked one on top of the other. The top tray held large rocks, then the next tray smaller rocks, and then finally a tray of fine sand.

What would happen when the unrefined oil was poured through each layer? It would become purified, without impurities or unwanted elements. Is the thing that attracts you to your fiancée her purified character? Or are there impurities in her life that you're explaining away—and that your parents from an uninvolved vantage point see as future problems?

If you know you've gotten your parents' blessing, and now they are very concerned about your loved one's character, it's time to step back, step into counseling, or otherwise slow down.

Does the timing seem right?

Another principle we can glean on genuine love from the Song of Songs is something Solomon's bride says repeatedly to a chorus of women. "Do not arouse or awaken love until it so desires" (Song of Songs 3:5). In other words, do not awaken love before its time.

Here comes the age-old issue of timing. I know a couple who dated for seven years steadily before getting married. I also met a couple who met during World War II at a coffee shop—spent four hours moving from small talk to talking seriously about marriage—then left the restaurant to find a Justice of the Peace! (By the way, they were married for forty-two years before the husband passed away, and their three sons are each in full-time ministry!)

If you come home after four hours at Denny's on a first date, and announce to a loving family you're engaged or just eloped—don't expect a warm reception. Even if your marriage does last forty years and your children grow up to serve the Lord, the biblical guideline is that given by Solomon's bride—"Don't awaken love before its time."

Don't hurry into something that you may regret at your leisure. And don't look for a parent's carte blanche blessing on your marriage if it's sudden, or a back-to-back rebound situation. Again, it may take time, and you should still go through a marriage preparation course to see the rosebud of love bloom in its time.

Are you speaking the same language?

Finally, make sure you and your parents are speaking the same language. If after one or two dates, you've come home and expressed, "I love him," you may be met with resistance. Not just because it's quick, but because your saying "I love him" may mean something far different than what they mean by "I love you."

Having feelings for someone isn't the same as loving them. Genuine love involves sacrifice, commitment, and unconditional acceptance. Perhaps the resistance you're getting from a parent is because when you say, "I love Dan," you're saying, "I think Dan's the type of person I *could possibly* love or marry." But they're hearing, "This is it! Dan's the man! I love him—as in sacrificial, forever, no-questions-asked lifelong commitment!"

Make sure you're talking the same language when you say you love the person you're dating. And then take stock of what we've said so far.

What Happens If:

1. You've honored your parents by listening carefully to their counsel on this person.
2. You're an independent adult, accepting responsibility, and, in most cases, living under your own roof.
3. You've received their blessing in the past.
4. You understand the positive side of their love as a reflection of their high value for you.
5. You have looked objectively at your loved one's character for flaws they may see that you don't.
6. You've waited a sufficient amount of time for love to bloom.
7. You are sure you and your parents are speaking the same language.

8. You are not breaking any biblical barriers (like marrying a non-Christian).

And your parents *still* don't agree on your choice of a life partner?

Now you're at your own three-foot putt. Let's say you've dated for a lengthy period, you are fully independent as an adult, you are confident of your loved one's commitment to Christ and their godly character, and you've made sure your parents know your definition of love isn't a feeling, but a lifelong commitment.

Perhaps your hard choice may be to marry without their blessing. Then again, it may be to share the material in this chapter with them, and wait. You're free to do either.

But what if you never did get your parents' blessing?

Path Two: If You Did Not Receive Your Parents' Blessing

We've looked at Stacy, above, who received her parents' blessing. But what if you're like another young woman named Kris, who never once got a positive, loving blessing from her parents? When I meet with people like her, I encourage them to face several key questions and issues.

Is this marriage an attempt to gain a gift you never received at home?

Kris grew up in a home with parents who were extreme perfectionists. She could never keep her room clean enough, get good enough grades, or bring home a potential suitor who measured up.

When she met James during her freshman year of college, she fell head-over-heels in love. For the first time, she'd met someone who consistently praised her achievements, told her she was attractive, and in many ways, provided the blessing she'd never gotten from her parents.

After six weeks at school, they were convinced they were in love. By Thanksgiving, she showed up at home with a trunk full of dirty clothes . . . and a fiancé.

When her parents objected to how quickly their relationship had moved from acquaintance to engagement, she dismissed their counsel as typically negative. Kris had found in her fiancé a level of acceptance—at least initially—that she'd never known with her parents.

Forget objectivity and her parents' concern. She was in a race to enter a perpetual state of marital bliss. Unfortunately, her marriage ended after a stormy year and a half, and she had to endure both the heartache of a broken relationship, and her parents' repeated digs, "We told you so!"

If you've missed the blessing at home, ask yourself a hard question, "Am I, in fact, rushing into a marriage to make up for missing the blessing?" Even if you've been dating the person for a significant amount of time, is the idea of leaving home more attractive than the person you're looking to marry? That's not to say that a spouse can't be a blessing. She can be a gift from God and fill much of the hole in your heart. But she can't fill it all, nor will she ever be your parents.

If you've come from a home where there was a significant lack of acceptance or caring actions, you need to face those hurts and missing needs directly. Otherwise, it can cloud your perspective and keep you from hearing clearly the concerns that the Lord—or your parents—may have with your relationship.

Once you've looked at your motivation for marriage, it's important to look at another issue.

Are there family rules you're breaking by marrying this person?

Bryan's grandfather was a precinct chairman for one particular political party. His father actually ran for party office. For three generations, no one in Bryan's family had voted anything other than a straight party-line ticket. Now Bryan had brought home the woman he felt should be his life partner—and she was from just as long a line of opposition party supporters.

The opposition Bryan faced to his marriage had little to do with who his fiancée was. It had almost everything to do with an

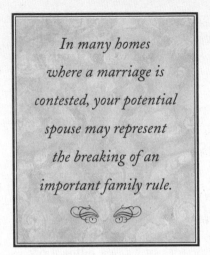

In many homes where a marriage is contested, your potential spouse may represent the breaking of an important family rule.

unwritten family rule that was being broken. Namely, he was bringing an enemy into the camp.

In many homes where a marriage is contested, your potential spouse may represent the breaking of an important family rule. Perhaps you come from a family that loves to camp and go to sporting activities. Then you bring home a fiancée who considers camping her least favorite activity, and sports a bore.

If you find the opposition to your potential spouse is because they've broken a cardinal family rule, ask yourself first, "Is this rule really biblical?" For example, if you're the only Christian in your family, and they're cool to your fiancée because he or she loves Jesus, breaking the rule of agnosticism or atheism can be expected. However, many family rules are much more subtle.

Ask yourself whether the opposition comes from a family rule your relationship is confronting.

Are you crossing a "distance/closeness" boundary?

A third issue to look at is whether your relationship crosses a family boundary.

In every home growing up, you find either "distance" or "closeness." Some families are and stay very close. You'll see them get together for weekly meals at Grandma's, give hugs and warm hellos when they meet, and maintain constant contact by phone. Other families are like a dorm room. Everyone lives in the same house, but they go their separate ways with very little connection.

If we're from an outgoing family who push involvement, and we're dating or engaged to someone who (because of a "distance" background) is standoffish and somewhat aloof—you can expect resistance. If you're warm and outgoing and find yourself marrying into a family that values distance and privacy, you may well meet resistance just by being who you are.

It's important as adults to look carefully at family expectations. Choosing to marry someone who isn't as outgoing or reserved as your family isn't wrong. However, over long years of holidays, family get-togethers, children and cousins, and so forth, look long and hard at the boundary you may be crossing. The cost of crossing that boundary (and the source of the resistance you're meeting) needs to be a significant consideration in whether to marry.

Is it loving protection—or unhealthy control?

I mentioned earlier that genuine love is protective. You wouldn't take your 1964 mint-condition Corvette and toss the keys to someone who has alcohol on his breath and a history of car wrecks. Loving parents can and should point out concerns with the priceless gift God has given them—you! However, in some families, protection is a form of control, not genuine caring.

If you come from a controlling home, I'd encourage you to read a book by Dr. Tim Kimmel called *Powerful Personalities* (Focus on the Family, 1994). It's a significant work that can help you deal with overly controlling people (and parents) without dishonoring them. In addition, if you're from a home where Mom and/or Dad made every decision and want control of your marriage decision as well, I'd recommend seeing a Christian pastor or counselor.

Often, people who grow up feeling unhealthily controlled make a stand at marriage. "You're not telling me what to do this time!" becomes a major motivation for marriage, not the merits of the person involved. To help sort out all the emotional issues involved in coming from a controlling home, I'd take Solomon's advice, "Many advisers make victory sure" (Proverbs 11:14).

Final Thoughts on a Difficult Decision

If you've missed your parents' blessing growing up, there are many factors to consider. We've looked at four:

- Are you trying to move out to gain a missing blessing?
- Are you breaking an unwritten family rule in marrying this person?
- Is there a distance/closeness perception at stake?
- Did you come from a very controlling home?

It's time for that "three-foot putt." And it's something I can't make for you. It would be my prayer that the issues raised in this chapter would help you take a next step. That step may be to talk to a Christian counselor or pastor. It may be to decide to wait for your parents' blessing before you take another step forward, or to realize that if your parents are non-Christians, they may never accept or bless your marrying a Christian.

I don't know your specific situation. But I do know that seeking the counsel of God's Word and wise individuals is crucial. Whatever your decision, it's better to err on the side of "going the extra mile" now to try to meet their objections and get their blessing, than to be dishonoring or rush into a decision that will have long-term consequences.

May the Lord bless you and give you his wisdom in the days to come!

8

Preparing for a Great First Year of Marriage

❧ H. Norman Wright ❧

Recently a couple in their mid-twenties shared this experience with me. They were supposed to attend a big Thanksgiving get-together, but the woman became quite ill, so she and her fiancé couldn't go. He came over and stayed around the clock for four days just helping her recover. Following the experience she said, "I was so surprised at his patience and sensitivity. I saw a new side to him that I didn't know was there. It was so reassuring."

This couple is well on their way to preparing for a great first year of marriage. They had taken the time to get to know each other well. They were committed to each other and to the goal of their future marriage. And their commitment and caring had stood up under several tests, including this illness.

Unfortunately, not all couples are so well prepared.

Wedding-Bell Blues

"I'm singing the blues." It's a line you would expect to hear from a cabaret singer, not a newlywed. After all, marriage is supposed to be the promised land where happiness abounds. Perhaps, but perhaps not. Listen to what this man said a few weeks after their wedding: "It's like I woke up one day, looked at Jean, and felt a knot in the pit of my stomach. She wasn't the person I thought she would be when we married, and now I think I've blown it. I married the wrong person. I feel terrible about this. Marriage wasn't supposed to be this way!"

About her first year of marriage a wife said, "The first year of our marriage was a disaster, at least for me. John wasn't anything like my father. When we were dating, in his eyes I couldn't do any wrong. After the honeymoon, I couldn't do anything right. He didn't like this, he didn't like that. And he is blunt and direct—no tact! There was no joy in marriage. What did I do wrong?" She was singing the "Wedding-Bell Blues." Disappointment, not happiness, was her prevailing feeling.

Is this normal? After the honeymoon, is this what to expect? Every couple will experience an adjustment after the honeymoon is over, and they settle into the first year of marriage.

When you are dating and in the courtship phase, you idealize each other. You're eager to find someone who shares your dreams, your goals, and your outlook on life. You focus on your similarities, what you have in common, and you pay little attention to your differences unless they are especially annoying. Love is blind, and even if you are aware of some bothersome qualities in your partner, you may not want to see them. So you overlook them because we're always supposed to look for the best in the other person, aren't we?

Another problem affects most couples—you either attribute to your fiancé special traits or qualities you wish were there (and really aren't), or he behaves in such a way to make you believe that's the way he is, when, in reality, he isn't. This is called "courtship deception." Are you getting what you think you're getting, or not?

The few months just before the wedding is a difficult time for a relationship. All the plans and details can place a strain on a relationship. But it can also distract you from confronting some of the potential problems and personality differences that can diminish the joy of your marriage. And when the wedding excitement is over and you do a reality check, it hits you hard.

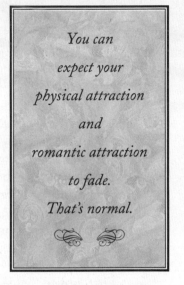

You can expect your physical attraction and romantic attraction to fade. That's normal.

Some call the first year of marriage the disappointment phase. That sounds pretty grim, doesn't it? For some it is. In fact, for many it is. A rash of divorces occur at the two-year mark in marriages and then again at the seven-year mark. For these couples, the wedding-bell blues turned into a death spiral. They entered marriage with high hopes and expectations. But they soon lost sight of the positive qualities of their partner and noticed only the negative ones. They see only the worst, imagine the worst, and create a negative vicious cycle.

Many couples based their decision to marry on physical love. This carries a marriage for about three to five years. Some based their marriage upon romantic love. This may carry a marriage along for five to seven years. If friendship love and agape love haven't developed, the relationship feels empty and can fall apart.

You can expect your physical attraction and romantic attraction to fade. That's normal. The lasting marriages are the ones where the couples built their love upon friendship and sacrificial love. In some ways, it's not really love that will hold your marriage together—it's commitment. This is a binding pledge or promise not only to the other person but to the marriage itself. As one husband said, when asked how their marriage had lasted so long, "We each had a commitment to each other and to the marriage. When our commitment to each other was low, it was the commitment to the marriage that kept us together."

Ways to Prevent the Wedding-Bell Blues

Commitment means giving up childish dreams and unrealistic expectations and accepting disappointments in marriage. Those who enter marriage unprepared for any problems, disappointments, or adjustments experience more of the wedding-bell blues than others. And the attitude you have toward your adjustments can make the difference.

So if you don't want to experience wedding-bell blues, what can you do now to prepare for a great first year of marriage?

Say Good-bye to the Single Life

First, realize that you can't bring your single lifestyle into your marriage. Some see marriage as just another addition to their already busy lifestyle. They think they'll just tack it on. It doesn't work that way. Some think they'll continue to play in their basketball league three nights a week or shop every Saturday with their mom as they've done for years. It won't work. Prior to your marriage, you need to identify all the changes you will be making in your life as well as what you will be giving up. You'll need literally to say good-bye to what you are giving up—and even grieve over it. And the older you are when you marry, the more work it will take on your part to make this adjustment.

Get to Know Your Future Spouse

Second, keep in mind that the person you marry (no matter who it is) is a foreigner. They will think differently, do things differently, behave differently, communicate differently, and even have some different values than you. But how much are you aware of this now? You need to learn to speak your partner's language, and they need to learn to speak yours.

One of your goals in your relationship is to know as thoroughly as possible your similarities and differences. You both need to come to the place where you can look at one another and say, "We are really different from one another. And it's okay for you to be you and for me to be me. We can learn from one another. These differences will help each of us become more flexible."

In order to fully know the other person, you need to see him or her

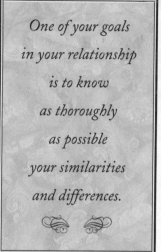

One of your goals in your relationship is to know as thoroughly as possible your similarities and differences.

outside of a dating relationship. Some of the following experiences have helped couples I've worked with:

- Go on a week's vacation with your partner and his or her parents.
- Work together on a project, or volunteer for a summer to work under adverse conditions at a Christian camp or on a mission trip.
- Put up Christmas tree lights on a house. (You have to be willing to give and take as well as cooperate.)
- Take care of the other person when he or she is sick.

How well do you really know your partner? The more you know who your partner really is, the less likely you are to experience the wedding-bell blues. Here are some basic questions for you to ask one another.

How did you get along with each of your parents? What were they like?

What did you like and dislike about your parents?

What was your birth order in your family?

How did you get along with your brothers and/or sisters?

Who were your favorite relatives?

What is the first thing that you can remember?

What special memories do you have of your childhood?

What do you remember about your first day of school?

What was your favorite grade and who were your favorite teachers?

What did you enjoy or dislike about school and its activities?

What were your hurts and disappointments as a child?

What were your hobbies and favorite games?

How did you usually get into trouble?

What pets did you have? Which were your favorites and why?

What did you dream about doing when you were older?

Did you like yourself as a child? Why or why not?

Did you like yourself as a teenager? Why or why not?

Did you have enough money in your youth? Enough clothing?

What were your talents and special abilities?

What awards and special achievements did you win?

Did you have a nickname?

Who were your close friends? Where are they today?

What would you do on a hot summer afternoon?

Describe the area where you grew up—people, neighborhood, etc.

What were you afraid of? Do you have any of those fears today?

At what age did you first like the opposite sex?

What was your first date?

Where did you go on dates?

How did you feel when you liked someone and that person didn't care for you?

Who were your other dates or steadies?

What did you like and dislike about each one?

What was your spiritual life like as a child? As an adolescent?

How has being an adult (nineteen on) changed your life?

How are you different today than you were ten years ago?

What have been your greatest disappointments? How have you handled them?

What have you learned from them that you would want me to learn?

What jobs have you held?

What is the extent of your education and job experiences?

What were your emotional reactions to jobs, fellow employees, and bosses?

What were your ambitions?

What do you think your natural gifts are?

What do you consider your strong points? Weak points?

What is your medical history?

What are your hobbies?

What is your definition of an ideal spouse?

Do you like pets? Which ones?

Who are the five most important people in your life?

Who are your friends now?

What is your church background?

Which Christian leaders or writers have influenced you?

Who were the Christians in your family?

Where would you like to live? What country, state, city, neighborhood, type of dwelling?

What are your views on aging?

What are your views on money?

What has been the best year of your life? Why?

Who educated you in sex?

What were your sexual experiences?

What is your standard for sexual expression at this time in your life?

What are your political views?

What do you enjoy reading? Watching on TV?

Have you ever had a child?

Do you want children?[1]

One of the greatest contributions to the blues are expectations. When you marry, you have a list of positive expectations.

> *The higher the level*
>
> *of expectations, the more*
>
> *idealistic the dreams,*
>
> *the less prepared*
>
> *you are for the onset*
>
> *of inevitable*
>
> *disillusionment.*

Who would ever enter marriage with negative ones? But many expectations are unrealistic. And they will lead not only to disappointment, but right into the marital death spiral.

"That Lovin' Feelin'"

Over the years, we have heard couples say they were not just disappointed with their partner, they've actually fallen out of love with them. This problem is totally avoidable! And if you are aware of the process and stages of falling out of love, you can not only keep it from happening but can create a marriage that is fulfilling. When love dies it goes through five stages.

Disillusionment

The first stage is *disillusionment*. Almost everyone who marries eventually experiences disillusionment. The higher the level of expectations, the more idealistic the dreams, the less prepared you are for this phase. When you don't expect or anticipate it, the devastation is worse.

In this first phase, you experience disappointment that moves to disenchantment with marriage itself. You compare your partner now with the way she was before you were married. Over the years I've heard many wives complain about the change they noticed in their husbands even during the first month of marriage. They said their husbands were open, feelings oriented, communicative, and highly attentive during their courtship, but that within a month, all that had disappeared.

Sometimes the partner has, in fact, changed, but other times it's only the perception you have of the other's behavior. What you used to see as positive traits are now viewed as negative. As one husband said, "I knew she was organized and neat, but not to this extent. She's so rigid and perfectionistic, it's hard to live with her."

When the negative feelings occur, thoughts that feed the disaffection process begin. At this phase, you are aware that the relationship isn't going as well as expected. This can lead to doubts about the person you married, as well as your decision to marry them.

Hurt

Hurt is the best way to describe the second phase of the death of love, which can overlap the first phase. The feelings in this phase include loneliness, the sense of being treated unfairly and unjustly, and a sense of loss. Often you don't identify your feelings as those of loss or perceive what the loss involves. Now the thoughts expand to include more negatives such as the following:

"My wife just doesn't understand me."

"My husband just isn't meeting my needs."

"I must not be very important to her, or she'd be acting differently."

You may begin to think about what the relationship is costing you compared to what you're getting out of it. Usually you feel you have ended up with the short end of the stick!

Your old nature begins to kick in. We all have a bent or inclination toward negative thinking. It's one of the effects of the Fall. You begin to use a gift that God has given you—the imagination—in a negative manner. We all talk to ourselves. But too often, unfortunately, the content is negative. You ignore the positive.

In this hurt phase, certain behaviors occur. To solve hurt feelings, you seek out a confidant in order to gripe and complain about how dissatisfying the marriage or partner is. You make attempts to change the relationship and make it better, and you try to change your partner as well. We can and need to help one another change in a healthy way. But when you're coming at the problem from a position of hurt, you usually use an approach that either reinforces the basic problem or makes it worse.

Anger

The third phase is *anger*. It too can overlap with the previous phase as a husband or wife travels the road to the loss of love. The disillusionment diminishes, and the hurt turns into anger.

Anger doesn't have to kill a marriage. It can actually show that you still care about your partner and the relationship. It can be a sign that you're alive and well and want to have something better in the relationship. Anger causes you to assert yourself in situations where you should. And if anger is handled correctly, it can actually be an invitation to negotiate.

But this is the time when the phrase, "I think I'm falling out of love," begins to emerge. As the disappointment and hurts continue, they obscure the love that was there when the relationship began.

With feelings and thoughts like this, you can imagine what behaviors might happen at this time. By now you are beginning to express feelings to your partner, not in a way that draws you closer, but in a way that alienates him. Expressions of hurt, anger, and disappointment are usually presented in a critical way, mingled with an air of disgust. It's not uncommon to avoid your partner; and sexual involvement is either cut off or becomes a mechanical duty. You withdraw physically, and emotionally you withdraw from both your partner and the marriage. As one wife said, "How is it possible to physically respond to someone you've started to loathe? I can't even sleep in the same bed with him because I'm so angry at him."

This is a dangerous time in your life, for hurt and anger will make you vulnerable to seeking fulfillment elsewhere. In the death of love, emotional desperation is usually present, which becomes a perfect breeding ground for affairs. This lack of fulfillment and intimacy creates an intense vacuum that contributes to alienation as well as resentment.

Ambivalence

The fourth phase of love's loss is *ambivalence*. Your feelings reflect a sense of turmoil, because they shift back and forth between despair and hope for both the marriage and your partner. You're indecisive and unsure about what to do. You wonder, *What will it take for this marriage to work?* and *Would it be best to just get out of this?* You consider other options to staying with your partner, but you also think about how the divorce would affect you and others.

All these feelings and thoughts lead to a set of behaviors that could include counseling. You might make friends and relatives aware of what is occurring. You begin to think about another person who might be a better choice than the current partner. Once again, remember that these phases can overlap, and it can all add up to one big state of confusion!

Disaffection

The final phase is what all this has been leading up to: *disaffection*, or the death of love. The only feelings left are those that reflect the death of what each hoped would be a happy and fulfilling relationship. Indifference, detachment, and apathy exist, and that's about it. I've heard this expressed in many ways:

"I've had it. I have no more energy. Nothing I did worked, and now it's over."

"I have nothing left to feel with. I'm numb. I never thought it would end up like this. But ten years is enough time to invest in a bankrupt situation."

"I can't even get angry at her anymore. There's nothing left, and I'm moving on."

"I don't care what she says she'll do now. It's too late. I don't even want to try anymore. I've been rejected way too much."[2]

No couple who marries ever wants something like this to happen. It's the worst-case scenario. You can avoid this tragedy if you remember what causes it: unrealistic expectations, the absence of friendship love developing in the relationship, one person being a controller, and the absence of emotional intimacy.

The remedy to all these toxins is found in your attitude. I recently counseled a woman who captured this attitude beautifully. She told me, "I knew there would be disappointments and that John had flaws. During the first two years these became more evident, and each time they emerged I just took the attitude of 'I knew this beforehand. I'm just discovering them now. It's all right. I couldn't handle a perfect man anyway, because he's got to live with me. And I've got lots of flaws.' I guess that's what love is all about . . . loving a flawed person. God knows all about that, too, doesn't he?"

Certainly he does. Yet God stays in love with us.

Getting Your Thinking Straight

What can you do to cultivate an attitude that will prevent wedding-bell blues and prepare you for a great first year of marriage? You can begin by each of you writing down at least twenty expectations you have for your potential partner as well as for the marriage itself. Then look at each list and answer the following questions:

1. Do we both have expectations in this area?
2. Do I have the same expectations for myself as I do for my fiancé? Why not?
3. How are our expectations of each other alike or different?
4. Whose expectations are stronger?
5. Whose expectations are most often met? Why? Because that person is older, stronger, more intelligent, male, more powerful?
6. Where do my expectations originate? From parents, books, church, siblings, the neighborhood where I grew up?
7. Are my expectations more worthy of fulfillment than my fiancé's?

8. Do all the people I know have the same expectations in a given area?
9. Do I have a "right" to my expectations?
10. Am I obligated to live up to my future spouse's expectations?[3]

Now take each expectation and answer the following:

1. Is this expectation I have of my fiancé supported by objective reality? Is it objectively true that he or she should act this way?
2. Am I hurt in any way, shape, or form if this expectation is not fulfilled?
3. Is this expectation essential to the attainment of any specific goal I have for my marriage?
4. What does this expectation do to my future spouse's perception of me?
5. Does this expectation help me achieve the kind of emotional responses I want for my spouse and me in marriage?

You need to evaluate and clarify everything. This includes food tastes, cooking styles, neatness level, time you retire at night and whether it's together or separately, taste in interior decoration, amount you spend on gifts, how important it is to you to remember birthdays and anniversaries, noise level in the home, frequency and type of TV programs, and so forth. These may sound mundane, but you wouldn't believe the number of marriages that fall apart because of these conflicts. If some item or issue isn't important or significant to you, but it is to your partner, then it needs to become more important to you. This is part of your growing and learning process.

As you approach marriage, take plenty of time now to get acquainted and build a quality friendship. The more you do now, the more prepared you will be to experience a great first year of marriage.

For Those Getting Married Again

❧ Tom Whiteman ❧

*I*t was a great idea: a Sunday school class for newly remarried couples. My church already had a successful divorce-recovery ministry well in place, but now some remarried couples were looking for support from others who were in the same boat. About a dozen couples joined the class, which I taught.

I hope this doesn't reflect on my teaching ability, but three of these couples divorced within four years of their remarriage, and another couple is practically separated. The sad fact is that remarriage is a difficult business.

Each of the couples had waited several years after their previous marriage before remarrying. And all of the couples had gone through a ten-week premarital class that included four weeks of couple's counseling.

In short, they probably had much more preparation for what they were about to face than the average couple entering marriage.

Yet in spite of all they had going for them, each of the couples expressed that they had grossly underestimated the amount of difficulty they would face in the first year of marriage. They consistently identified the areas of greatest conflict as "blending the children" and "baggage from the past."

> *The greatest areas of conflict in remarriage are (1) blending the children and (2) baggage from the past.*

"Without the kids," one of them told me, "perhaps we could have worked through our difficulties. But with them playing one against the other and deliberately sabotaging our relationship, it was more than we could bear."

Another couple knew full well how difficult it would be to handle the children. He was a social worker, well read on the do's and don'ts of blending a family. Before he even considered remarriage, he made sure his two children grew to respect and love the woman he married. "But after we got back from the honeymoon," he said later, "everything changed. At first the kids were quiet and withdrawn. But then my wife began to resent their behavior, and before I knew it, they were at each other's throats. And then I was drawn into the battle. My wife, who could not handle the constant turmoil, left. She feels that I chose my kids over her."

For a third couple, the ex-wife became an issue. Mike remained rather friendly with his first wife, Janice. That was fine with Claire, his new wife—as long as Janice kept her distance. But Janice was often calling to ask Mike to come over and help with a problem with the kids, or the sink, or the finances. As a Christian, Mike felt he had an obligation to treat his former wife with love and respect, but Claire felt neglected and mistreated.

Getting married again, especially with children, is much more complex than a first-time marriage. Therefore, before you

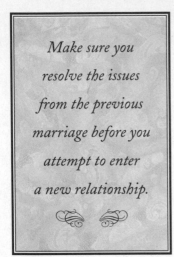

Make sure you resolve the issues from the previous marriage before you attempt to enter a new relationship.

consider such an undertaking, you need to take a serious look at a number of issues that don't often come up in normal marriage counseling. I put these issues in four major categories: *resolving, renewing, reconnecting,* and *recommitting.*

Resolving

Have the issues of the previous marriage been resolved?

This is the most important question to ask as you approach a remarriage, whether the previous marriage ended in death or divorce. In either case, you need to grieve. Unless you are well healed from that grief, you will have serious trouble in a new relationship.

Over eighty percent of divorced people will remarry, many before they are ready.[1] Research indicates that it takes anywhere from two to five years to grieve the loss of a marriage partner.[2] For some divorcing people, the turmoil can last longer than five years.

During the time of adjustment, people go through well-defined stages of grieving that include denial, anger, bargaining, depression, acceptance, and forgiveness.[3] During this period of emotional adjustment, people are quite vulnerable to a "rescuing relationship"—someone who will take them away from the mess and help them get back on their feet.

Following my own divorce some eighteen years ago, I sensed this same need. For about two years I remained isolated from others, feeling very sorry for myself and alone. My life consisted of unfulfilling work, lonely nights, and cereal. Yes, cereal. For breakfast and dinner, I had cereal because it was quick and easy. I had little energy to take care of myself, or to care for anyone else.

I eventually realized that I needed to get out again and circulate with others. I attended a local singles group where I found some very exciting, but threatening, situations. People were friendly and nice to me, but they asked me extremely embarrassing questions—such as "How are you doing?" I wanted to run back home and isolate myself again. But I didn't. I stayed. And very quickly I began to heal and grow stronger.

One Sunday a beautiful young woman began to pay attention to me. She was asking me about myself and eventually invited me over for Sunday brunch. I felt as if I had died and gone to heaven. For years I had felt unwanted and unloved. Now, here was this woman who seemed to find me interesting. And then she fed me—real food, not just cereal! You can see how easily I might fall in love and assume that this woman was an angel sent by God to rescue me from my lonely fate. Perhaps this was God's way of giving me back all that I had lost.

But it was not to be. I was not ready yet. I still had a lot of healing to do, and a lot of issues to resolve. Fortunately for both of us, she recognized that. I was devastated once again, but she spared me a fate much worse.

Many will remarry in this vulnerable state. They may feel ecstatic about the new relationship, and great about themselves, but their emotional high is masking an underlying emptiness that only time and personal growth can fill.

I waited another six years before I remarried. When I did, I was not desperate or lonely. Nor was I eating cereal. I had developed some wonderful friendships. I had a very satisfying job and lifestyle, and I had learned how to barbecue steak really well.

How can you tell when you have resolved all of your issues from the past? I can't speak specifically to your situation. For that, I would highly recommend premarital counseling with someone who understands second marriages. I can, however, provide you with a general checklist.

____ I have grieved the loss of my former spouse and given myself at least two years to heal. (This is a minimum. Perhaps even more time is needed.)

____ I have been able to forgive those who hurt me, let me down, or disappointed me during my time of crisis. (True forgiveness means you are now able to wish them well and mean it!)

____ I have resolved past guilt, and I have sought forgiveness from God and from others (especially my former spouse) for the things that I did wrong in my previous relationship.

____ My children have also been able to forgive and heal the past hurts.

____ My children are able to love both of their parents, and we are able to co-parent in a healthy way.

____ I have learned to be content as a single, as a single parent, or as an absentee parent. I am not seeking remarriage to find a better life for me or my children.

____ I understand what I contributed to the breakup of my former marriage, and I have worked at changing this unhealthy pattern or tendency. (If widowed, you still need to identify the unhealthy aspects of your former marriage. If you can't come up with anything you did wrong in your former relationship, then you are bound to repeat mistakes of the past.)

Renewing

After *resolving* the baggage from the past, you need to *renew* yourself and your children.

As you sorted through your past issues, you identified habits and patterns that damaged your previous marriage, not only your former spouse's behavior, but also your own. Yet recognizing what you did wrong does not solve the problem. Now you have to change those bad habits, replacing them with healthy *new* patterns.

Say, for example, that my part in the breakup of my marriage was insensitivity and lack of meaningful communication with my former wife. Recognizing that fact does not make me a better communicator. Now I have to examine where that pattern came from, understand the triggers and circumstances that feed the pattern, and then take steps to change it. That could take a fairly long time.

Renewal also involves rebuilding your sense of self—spiritually, emotionally, and mentally. *Who are you?* Divorce can do a number on your self-esteem (and, in a different way, so can bereavement). You need to discover a balanced self-image that embraces your value as a flawed but beloved child of God.

How will you know when you have been fully renewed? Good question. I believe *contentment* is the key. If you can

> *You are not truly ready to remarry until you are happy being single.*
> ❦ ❦

reach a point of satisfaction about where you are in life, that's a sign that renewal has taken place. There is some irony here. You are not truly ready to remarry until you are happy being single.

Many assume just the opposite. They feel that unhappiness with the single life and a frantic desire to be married again are signs that God *wants* them to remarry. But I strongly believe these are signs that renewal has not occurred. Any remarriage at this point would be in serious trouble from the start.

In the early days of my single-again experience, I had many lonely days and nights. I also thought, "I can't go on like this. I've *got* to find someone I can share my life with." The thought of being alone for even one year was unthinkable (if you told me it would be eight years before my remarriage, I'd have screamed to high heaven!). Yet the longer I was alone, and the healthier I became, the easier the days and nights became.

I remember a moment about five years after my first wife left me. I thought, *What if I'm single for the rest of my life?* This thought had crossed my mind before, always making me shudder. But this time was different. I simply shrugged and said, "That would be okay." Being single for the rest of my life was not what I desired, but I had finally learned to be content with where God had me! That was a great feeling.

You may remember Paul's assertion that he had "learned to be content whatever the circumstances . . . in any and every situation" (Philippians 4:11–12). Such contentment is the key to the personal renewal that's necessary before you remarry.

There are many wrong reasons to get married again, some of which I've gathered on this checklist. While few would admit these are *primary* reasons for remarrying, they often come into play. Which of these apply to you?

Check all those that might be part of your motive to remarry:

____ I'm lonely.

____ My children need a mother/father.

____ I need financial help.

____ I'm sexually frustrated.

____ I could use the help around the house.

____ My lifestyle is hectic or depressing.

A remarriage may temporarily fix some of these problems, but it will certainly create even more problems. Take the time to renew your life, your self-image, and your spirit before you consider another marriage.

Reconnecting

Once your life has been *renewed*, then you're ready to begin *reconnecting* with others. If you're engaged or in a serious relationship, you may assume that you've already reconnected sufficiently. But you may have sidestepped a few essential areas. There are two crucial types of reconnecting: (1) with the past; and (2) in new relationships.

Reconnecting with the Past

When a marriage breaks up, many other relationships often break, too. Families are torn apart. Friends choose sides or drift away. Even longtime friends from church often avoid you in the wake of a divorce.

Reconnecting means going to those people, forgiving their wrongs (and asking forgiveness for yours), and restoring some kind of relationship (even if it can never be the same as it was).

If you have children, that's where you should start. Then try to reconnect with other family members and close friends who may have drifted away. Some of these friendships will need to remain distant—for instance, your former in-laws can't be expected to have the same place in your life as before—but the reestablishment of a cordial spirit will be crucial to the success of future relationships.

Unresolved issues from the past have a way of haunting us in the future. That's why you must learn to let go of the rancor you feel toward those who have let you down. This is probably most crucial, and yet hardest to accomplish, with your former spouse.

Many assume that it's best to make a clean break, never speaking with your former spouse again. But relationship research seems to concur with biblical teaching (Matthew 18:15–17), indicating that it's healthiest to clear up old disputes. Any new relationship will benefit from this, and it's very important if there are children from that previous marriage.

Nancy recently married Brad, who had a daughter from a tempestuous first marriage. Brad had barely spoken to his former wife in years, since they couldn't seem to talk without arguing. The daughter, Michelle, visited Brad and Nancy every other week-end—and Brad was thankful when she was old enough to drive. He didn't want to deal with his ex any more than he had to.

This seemed like a good situation to Nancy, who assumed that Brad's avoidance of his former wife would keep any old issues from creeping into their new marriage. But then Michelle started getting into trouble in school. Brad and Nancy knew they needed to coordinate any disciplinary efforts with Michelle's mom, but Brad still didn't want to talk with her. So they ended up sending messages through Michelle. Bad idea. The messages always got twisted, and they got some nasty messages back.

Finally Nancy decided it was time to put an end to this nonsense. She picked up the phone to call Brad's ex.

"Don't do that!" Brad exclaimed. "It will only make things worse. Believe me, I've dealt with this woman for years. You have no idea how miserable she can make your life."

So she put down the phone, but things only got worse. That's when she called me, and I advised her to call Michelle's mom. She did.

With Brad sweating bullets in the next room, his new wife talked with his old wife for two hours, clearing up misunderstandings, discussing Michelle's well-being, and setting new boundaries for the relationship. Regular communication was established, and it continues to this day. While there are still glitches at times, things have been steadily improving.

Reconnecting does not mean you have to be good friends, or that you excuse all the painful deeds of the past. It does mean that you reopen the lines of communication. Ideally, you can come to forgive those who hurt you, wishing them well, even at a distance. It also means that you learn to cooperate for the best interest of your children.

If you make attempts at reconnecting and the other person refuses, then you can move on, knowing that at least you tried to do the right thing. You are not responsible for the other person's reaction.

Reconnecting in New Relationships

After divorce or the death of a spouse, most people find that they need a new support system, perhaps a new church or set of friends. The person who was closest to you is now gone, and many other relationships may also be damaged. You will probably need new friendships, in which you can try out your new, healthier patterns of relating.

I recommend that people first reconnect in same-sex friendships.[4] Relationships with the opposite sex are too complicated for you right now. Your new friend could easily take the place of your former spouse in any number of ways, and you're not ready yet for a new romance. This doesn't mean you shouldn't speak with anyone of the opposite sex, but be careful to avoid close friendships that might turn romantic.

I recommend that people first reconnect in same-sex friendships.

I remember how long it took for me to find a new friend I could trust. I turned to some old friends, but many of them were married—and that was now a very different lifestyle from mine. I needed a single male who could provide weekend support, entertainment, and accountability. Fortunately, I found a couple of friends like that. These friendships helped me to develop the confidence I needed to move into other relationships. In this safe environment, I learned much more about sharing, caring, and commitment.

The next level of my reconnecting involved dating. Except now my dating was deliberately slow, and with a heavy emphasis on *relating*, *communicating*, and *developing friendship*. If you are moving toward marriage, make sure you have not skipped these important steps. You may find that when the infatuation wears off, you have very little in common.

Recommitting

The final stage in moving toward remarriage is to learn how to trust and to commit again. This is a huge step for most people. Whether your marriage ended by death or divorce, your heart has been seriously wounded. You're not eager to put it in danger again.

This often creates a tug-of-war: you desperately want to reconnect with someone, but you're afraid you'll get hurt again.

I find that many remarrying couples face this just before or after engagement. They've moved enthusiastically into each other's life, but now they start to wonder, "How do I know if she will always love me?" "What if he finds someone else?" "How do I know he won't leave me like my last husband?" "Can I entrust my wounded heart to her?" Many get cold feet and break the engagement, or they suddenly draw up prenuptial agreements, or they decide to move on in the relationship—but with great fear and trepidation.

I had lost my first home in my divorce. It had taken me five years to get back on my feet financially. I was proud of my ability to recoup my losses, and I reveled in my new independence. So as I dated Lori, who later became my wife, I thought about how hard it would be to surrender my home, my belongings, and my financial independence over to someone else. Little by little I began to let go of possessions for the sake of the relationship. But even after our engagement, I cringed at the thought of allowing joint ownership of my house. Was this selfish? Probably. Was it wrong? Perhaps, but it was also a very natural reaction. Since I'd felt betrayed in a previous marriage, I was careful not to be hurt in the same way again.

Lori was very understanding and patient, not pushing me at all. This helped me to work through these issues in my mind and resolve them.

That may be a key issue in learning recommitment. The wounded heart has to heal properly before a person takes another chance. Pressure or pushing usually only makes things worse.

But ultimately every marriage involves taking a leap of faith. Is there any guarantee that your spouse will always love you and never leave you? No, there's always that chance. We hope our love does not blind us to that possibility, but provides the reasonable faith to take that leap.

Commitment and trust continue to be issues well after the wedding, because the intimate nature of marriage brings out issues that have lain buried since the previous relationship ended.

One man who had a problem with anger in his first marriage worked on this issue in counseling for several years. Then he slowly rebuilt new relationships and spent several more years demonstrating healthier patterns in his dating. Yet when he finally married, he admitted that this was the first real test of his ability to react differently.

"I found some of my angry patterns returning," he told me, "but this time I sought help right away before it got out of hand." He thought he had defeated this beast, but his new marriage revived it. Fortunately, he beat it again.

Trust became an issue in my first marriage. And, even after I learned to trust Lori in our two years of dating, the same issue popped up early in *our* marriage. Lori went shopping one Saturday afternoon, saying she'd be back around dinnertime. When she wasn't home by five, I started looking for her. By 5:30, I was pacing the floor, mumbling to myself about her whereabouts. By 5:45 I was really upset. "She said she'd be home at dinnertime, so *where is she?*"

When Lori strolled in at around six, eager to show off her purchases, I was in a foul mood. "Where were you! You said . . . Why didn't you call? . . . You could have been *dead* somewhere, for all I knew!"

Lori calmly set down her packages and looked at me rather strangely. "I think there's someone here with us!" she said.

I looked around the empty room. What was she talking about?

"I think it's your ex-wife," she explained. "From the way you're reacting—no, overreacting—this has to be about more than me coming home a little late."

I was stunned for a few moments. But soon I realized she was exactly right. The incident reminded me of feelings I had in my previous marriage. Whenever my former wife was out late, I had no idea where she was, but I had a pretty good idea she was cheating on me. It caused me a lot of pain. Only in my remarriage did these feelings return.

Trust and commitment are ongoing issues in marriage. Before you remarry, make sure you have thoroughly dealt with the difficult issue of recommitting yourself in a new relationship.

Conclusion

If you are approaching remarriage, you're about to embark on one of life's most challenging journeys. You have learned to love again, but will you be able to trust? Will you win the love of your spouse's children? Will you successfully blend two very different families? These and a thousand other questions will have to be resolved. But with the help of God, a lot of patience, flexibility, and a determination to succeed, you can experience the joy of a fresh start—a second chance at love, family, and happiness.

10

After the Honeymoon

❧ Les and Leslie Parrott ❧

We've got to be honest: Your love life is at risk. Oh, sure, you're crazy in love now and you can't imagine that anything will change. We pray it won't. But it wouldn't be fair to close this book without letting you know the truth. If recent divorce and remarriage statistics are any indication, being married does not ensure a life of love lived happily ever after. Contrary to the fairy tales we were weaned on, romance always runs the risk of fading. No, let us rephrase that—romance always fades. As human beings, we aren't built to maintain the high levels of feverish passion and romance experienced during the days of engagement and the honeymoon. And yet that's exactly what most couples expect.

Even the more mature stories of doomed love reinforce this notion. Remember the tragic twosome Romeo and Juliet? How about Lancelot and Guinevere? Rhett and Scarlett? Each snuffed out their powerful love while the heat of passion was turned up full blast. Why? Because it couldn't last. The heat of passion was never meant to. Can you imagine Romeo and Juliet as a married couple ... going off to work ... paying bills ... grocery shopping? It's almost incongruous; at least it takes a lot of the luster off their love story. The point is that all the romancing and wooing that led up to your marriage is not what will sustain it. Not in real life.

You can't expect your marriages to be long-running cinematic fairy tales. Those couples who hold on to this faulty expectation end up drinking the "poison" of adultery or trading in partners to reinvent the fantasy, hoping that this time they'll get it right. But rest assured. There's a better way.

In this final chapter we reveal a once-in-a-lifetime opportunity you have as newlyweds to put into practice the secret for a wildly successful love life that will go the distance. And we suggest a three-step plan for making it a lasting reality.

The Secret of Lasting Love

When they married eighteen months ago, Kim never would have dreamed she'd find herself complaining that her husband Steve didn't show her enough affection. "He was so attentive that he would notice if I changed a part in my hair or bought a new blouse," Kim says. But the loving words and compliments come a little less often now, and frankly, Kim misses the special attention. "He thinks I'm the one who's cooling off," she shrugs, "but I just can't get interested in sex when I feel I'm being ignored."

Kim and Steve aren't alone. The frequent expressions of affection and approval that couples give each other during the courtship and honeymoon stage can dwindle during the first years of marriage. You may love each other as much, but you tend to talk about it less. There's a peak of emotional intimacy during the early phase of a relationship and then the "I love yous" dwindle and the romance fades. The good news is that if you know the secret, you can keep romantic love alive long after the honeymoon has ended. What's the secret? It's quite simple, really: *Do everything you can in your first year of marriage to establish habits of loving behavior.*

A Three-Step Post-Honeymoon Plan

A habit is a recurrent, often unconscious pattern of behavior that is acquired through frequent repetition. If you repeat a behavior often enough, it becomes a pattern. Eventually, you hardly give it a thought.

The little things you do now will cut a groove in your relationship that will likely last a lifetime.

The behavior becomes second nature. Whether it be fastening a safety belt when you get in a car or biting your fingernails to pass the time, habits shape our actions. According to seventeenth-century English writer Jeremy Taylor, "Habits are the daughters of action." And habits can bring about either positive or negative action. They can lead to behaviors that cultivate and nurture lasting love, or they can lead to behaviors that serve as love's saboteur. Most importantly, once a habit is "set," it's next to impossible to break—no matter how nasty or dangerous it is. Just ask a chain-smoker.

Why all this talk about habits? Because you are at an important developmental passage where what you do in the next few months will determine many of the habits you have for the rest of your marriage. The little things you do now—without thinking—will cut a groove in your relationship that will likely last a lifetime. So we urge you to take charge of your romantic destiny. Establish patterns of loving behavior that will keep romance, passion, and intimacy alive and well in your marriage. Consider behaviors both big (how you spend your holidays) and small (how you greet each other at the end of the day). In fact,

One of the first things to go in a new marriage is politeness.

we will help you do just that in our three-step post-honeymoon plan for cultivating lasting love.

Step One: Note the Little Things

Have you ever been bit by an elephant? Chances are you haven't. Have you ever been bit by a mosquito? Probably. It's a silly illustration, but it makes a point: Little things often matter most. Especially in marriage. Too often, we think on a grand scale about romance—creating the perfect once-a-year getaway —and neglect the little opportunities that present themselves every day in marriage.

Consider, for example, how you greet one another when returning home from work. If you begin by making a consistent effort to reconnect with a tender touch or embrace at the end of your day, you will establish one of the most important patterns couples can have for setting a positive tone for their evening together. "Well, of course we'll do that," you may be thinking. Don't be so sure. The vast majority of couples end up with what researchers call the "grocery list" connection: "Did you pick up my dry cleaning?" "I'll need the car tomorrow." "What's for dinner?" If you start with a tender touch when you get home before you get to the nitty-gritty tasks of the day, you will create an aura of love in your home that leads to a level of fulfillment most married couples only dream about. Sure, it's a little thing, but a tender reconnection at the end of your day makes a huge difference when it becomes a habit.

Other "little things" to consider include common courtesies like saying *please* and *thank you*. Did you know that one of the first things to go in a new marriage is politeness? In some ways this reflects increasing levels of comfort. But if left unchecked, it can lead to rudeness. One study revealed that when paired with a stranger, even newlyweds were more polite to him or her than they were toward each other. If you establish a pattern of politeness now, you'll likely be even more polite on your fiftieth wedding anniversary!

Step Two: Make Dating a Habit

Many married couples claim they spend time together. But when you question them, you find they are spending that time running errands or meeting with other friends. There's

> *You need to have quality time together, just the two of you, when you have no other agenda except to connect.*

nothing wrong with that, of course, but if you are to keep romance alive, you need to have quality time together, just the two of you, when you have no other agenda except to connect. Some married couples call it their date night. And that's not a bad title. After all, there is no rule that says dating ends when you get married. In fact, dating becomes as important as ever after you've said your vows and settled into being a permanent couple. Whatever you call it, this time needs to be scheduled—routinely and consistently.

Every Thursday evening, for example, you need to be able to count on having a date: a leisurely dinner at your favorite restaurant, window-shopping downtown, a picnic at a local park, taking in a movie and ice cream, dressing up for a special event. Do whatever you enjoyed doing before you were married. The point of making dating a habit is to keep your marriage from falling into the doldrums of working all week and collapsing on the weekends. This toxic pattern has snuffed out the romantic flame of more couples than you can imagine. Don't let it happen to you.

In addition to scheduling a weekly time for just the two of you to be alone together, consider one overnight stay at a hotel every four months and a one-week vacation every year. By the way, once kids enter the picture, these romantic interludes become all the more essential. And if you don't establish the pattern of dating now, while you are just starting out, you are unlikely to do so when your lives become all the more hectic.

Step Three: Find a Marriage Mentor

Several years ago in Seattle, we started something we call The Marriage Mentor Club. We now have more than six hundred members in our city and several thousand across the country. The idea of marriage mentoring is so simple we're amazed that more couples don't do it. Mentoring begins by asking a seasoned, experienced, happy couple (not related to you) to come alongside you and invest in your relationship for the first year of your marriage. It doesn't have to be a big commitment. You may only meet with them three or four times. And you'd be amazed at how willing and honored a couple like this is to be invited to mentor you.

You might be wondering what a mentor couple can do for you? The answer is plenty. With years of experience, marriage mentors serve as a sounding board to help you navigate predictable passages like setting up your home, managing your finances, negotiating your different roles, managing conflict, dealing with in-law relations, preparing for holidays, and so on. Don't think of them as counselors. Mentors are more like your personal consultants or coaches. They will show you what's worked or hasn't worked for them—so you can learn from their mistakes instead of making your own.

Maybe you had excellent premarital counseling and expect to sail through your first year without a hitch. Maybe you will. But in our years of doing premarriage work with countless couples, we've discovered an experience that is almost predictable. We call it the "threshold phenomenon." It has to do with how different things look to a newlywed couple once they are actually married. The skills and techniques we taught them before they crossed the proverbial threshold seemed to have vanished. Actually, they never really took root in the first place. Why? Consider this analogy: If someone teaches you how to use a computerized spreadsheet when you have no reason to use it, you will probably tune out within the first few seconds. It's not relevant. Once you take a job, however, that requires you to use that same program, you are ready to learn. The same is true in the first year of marriage and a mentor couple can help you put into practice the things you already learned but have forgotten.

We know of few experiences that can help you more in your first married year than having a seasoned couple come alongside you and allow you to peer into their relationship so that you might lay a solid foundation for lasting love. If you would like to explore this idea of finding another couple to mentor you, begin by contacting your local pastor. The church you attend or one near where you live may have a mentoring program you can plug into. If not, you might ask the church to consider starting one. They can contact us to learn more about how to do this and we will send them the information about our *Mentoring Engaged and Newlywed Couples* video kit. Have them write to: Drs. Les and Leslie Parrott, Center for Relationship Development, Seattle Pacific University, Seattle, WA 98119.

The Honeymoon Habit

Over the years many couples return to the place of their first wedding trip for a second, third, or fourth honeymoon. Many couples work hard to recapture the bliss of their first few days as a couple. Perhaps you'll do the same. But don't wait for an anniversary or special occasion to recreate that special time. Keep love alive—starting today—by establishing daily habits of romance, passion, and intimacy. If you do, your honeymoon will become more than a memory. It will become a way of life.

Notes

Chapter 1: How to Know When You're Ready for Marriage

[1] E. H. Walster, "The Effects of Self-Esteem on Romantic Liking," *Journal of Experimental and Social Psychology* 1 (1965): 184–97.

[2] S. Sprecher and D. Felmlee, "The Influence of Parents and Friends on the Quality and Stability of Romantic Relationships: A Three-Wave Longitudinal Investigation," *Journal of Marriage and the Family* 54 (1992): 888–900.

[3] S. J. Katz and A. E. Liu, *False Love and Other Romantic Illusions: Why Love Goes Wrong and How to Make It Right* (New York: Ticknor and Fields, 1988).

[4] B. Lott, *Women's Lives: Themes and Variations in Gender Learning* (Monterey, Calif.: Brooks/Cole, 1987).

[5] N. G. Bennett, D. E. Bloom, and C. K. Miller, "The Influence of Nonmarital Childbearing on the Formation of First Marriage," *Demography* 32 (1995): 47–62.

[6] R. M. Cate and S. A. Lloyd, *Courtship* (Newbury Park, Calif.: Sage, 1992).

[7] K. Bradsher, "Young Men Pressed to Wed for Success," *New York Times*, December 13, 1989.

[8] J. F. Crosby, *Illusion and Disillusion: The Self in Love and Marriage*, 4th ed. (Belmont, Calif.: Wadsworth, 1991).

[9] D. H. Knox, Jr., *Marriage; Who? When? Why?* (Englewood Cliffs, N.J.: Prentice-Hall, 1975).

[10] H. Hendrix, *Getting the Love You Want* (New York: Henry Holt and Co., 1988), 36.

[11] K. Grover, "Mate Selection Processes and Marital Satisfaction," *Family Relations* 34 (1985): 383–86. Quoted in Neil Clark Warren's *Finding the Love of Your Life* (Colorado Springs: Focus on the Family, 1992).

[12] S. White and C. Hatcher, "Couple Complementarity and Similarity: A Review of the Literature," *American Journal of Family Therapy* 12 (1984): 15–25.

[13] Note: Among couples having age differences of ten years or fewer, there are very few significant differences in marital quality. How-

ever, in marriages in which the husband is eleven or more years older than his wife, marital problems concerning money, friends, etc. are more likely. H. Vera, D. Berardo, and F. Berardo, "Age Heterogamy in Marriage," *Journal of Marriage and the Family* 47 (1985): 553–66.

Chapter 2: Secrets of a Great Engagement

[1]For a more detailed discussion of how to appreciate your differences see "Date 5, Finding Unity in Your Diversity," in our book *Ten Great Dates to Revitalize Your Marriage* (Grand Rapids: Zondervan, 1997.)

Chapter 6: How to Have a Great Wedding Night

[1]Joseph Dillow, *Solomon on Sex* (Nashville: Thomas Nelson, 1977), 24–25.

[2]Paul Popenoe, *Preparing for Marriage* (Los Angeles: American Institute of Family Relations, 1951).

[3]Dillow, *Solomon on Sex*, 24–25.

[4]This chapter has been quoted from and adapted with written permission from *Getting Your Sex Life Off to a Great Start* by Clifford and Joyce Penner (Dallas: Word, 1994).

Chapter 8: Preparing for a Great First Year of Marriage

[1]Jim Smoke, *Facing 50* (Nashville: Thomas Nelson, 1994), 40–41.

[2]H. Norman Wright, *Finding Your Perfect Mate* (Eugene, Ore.: Harvest House, 1995), 253–54.

[3]H. Norman Wright, *Secrets of a Lasting Marriage* (Ventura, Calif.: Regal Books, 1995), chapter 3.

Chapter 9: For Those Getting Married Again

[1]Elizabeth Einstein and Linda Albert, *Preparing for Remarriage* (Stepfamily Living Series, 1983), 3–6.

[2]Judith Wallerstein, *Second Chances* (New York: Ticknor and Fields, 1989).

[3]See the *Fresh Start Divorce Recovery Workbook* by Burns and Whiteman, for a more extensive treatment of this process.

[4]Unless, of course, you are struggling with homosexuality. The point is that you need to develop friendships that are not sexual in nature, with no possibility of sexual attraction.

About the Authors

David and Claudia Arp are cofounders of Marriage Alive seminars and hosts of the nationally syndicated radio program, "The Family Workshop." Their numerous books include the Gold Medallion Award-winning *The Second Half of Marriage; Where the Wild Strawberries Grow;* and their book and video resource *10 Great Dates to Revitalize Your Marriage*. Dave and Claudia have served as columnists for *Christian Parenting Today* and have published articles in magazines such as *Today's Christian Woman, Virtue,* and *Marriage Partnership*. They have been married for thirty-five years and live in Knoxville, Tennessee.

Robert and Rosemary Barnes have been married since 1974 and have two children, Torrey and Robey. Bob is the director of Sheridan House Family Ministries, which includes a residential treatment center for teenage boys and girls, a social service center offering food, clothing, furniture, and automobiles to over nine hundred single moms a year, and a marriage and family counseling center. Rosemary is a retired public school teacher. Together, Bob and Rosemary have authored nine books on the family, including *Raising Confident Kids, Who's in Charge Here, Rock Solid Marriage, Great Sexpectations,* and *Ready for Responsibility*. Bob and Rosemary are frequent conference speakers and are the hosts of a weekly radio program called "Family Time."

Ron Blue is the founder and managing partner of Ronald Blue & Co., a fee-only financial planning firm. The firm offers financial planning, investment management, and tax and business services to individuals and organizations throughout the United States. Ron is the author of seven books on personal finance, including *Master Your Money* and *Generous Living*. He and his wife, Judy, are coauthors of *Raising Money-Smart Kids* and *A Woman's Guide to Financial Peace of Mind*. In addition, Ron is a special guest on numerous radio programs, and is a featured speaker with Promise Keepers. Residents of Atlanta, Georgia, Ron and Judy have five children and three grandchildren.

Les and Leslie Parrott not only share the same name, but the same passion for helping others build healthy relationships. In 1991, the Parrotts founded the Center for Relationship Development on the campus of Seattle Pacific University—a groundbreaking program dedicated to teaching the basics of good relationships. Married in 1984, the Parrotts' books include *Becoming Soul Mates, Questions Couples Ask, The Marriage Mentor Manual,* and the award-winning *Saving Your Marriage Before It Starts.* In addition to their many articles in *Marriage Partnership, Bride's, Focus on the Family,* and other magazines, their work has been featured in *USA Today* and *The New York Times* as well as on CNN, *Good Morning America,* and *The Oprah Winfrey Show.*

Clifford and Joyce Penner are internationally recognized sexual therapists, educators, and authors. Joyce is a registered nurse and clinical nurse specialist, while Cliff is a clinical psychologist. They work together as a team to counsel couples, teach sex education within school systems, lead sexual enhancement weekends for couples, lecture on human sexuality, and train fellow professionals. In addition to a full-time practice in sex therapy, the Penners have authored seven books including *Getting Your Sex Life Off to a Great Start, 52 Ways to Have Fun-Fantastic Sex, Men and Sex,* and the popular *The Gift of Sex: A Couple's Guide to Sexual Fulfillment.* Cliff and Joyce have also produced a four-hour video series: *The Magic and Mystery of Sex.* This series is designed for couples to use in enhancing their sexual communication as they learn more about their sexual lives together.

David and Jan Stoop have been married for more than forty years. Dave is a clinical psychologist with a private practice in Orange, California. He has served as an associate professor of psychology and marriage and family therapy in the Graduate School of Psychology at Fuller Seminary. Jan is a frequent speaker at women's groups and is a doctoral candidate in clinical psychology. Together, the Stoops have authored or coauthored fifteen books, including *Making Peace with Your Father; Forgiving Our Parents, Forgiving Ourselves; Self-Talk, Key to Personal Growth;* and *Seeking God Together: Spiritual Intimacy in Marriage.* Dave and Jan have three sons and three grandchildren, and live in Newport Beach, California.

John Trent is nationally recognized as a leading spokesman for the family. He is a frequent speaker at Promise Keepers conferences, and teaches relationship seminars across the country. Dr. Trent is also the author or coauthor of more than a dozen books on marriage and family relationships, including *The Gift of the Blessing*, and has won four Gold Medallion Awards, the Christian publishing industry's highest award for literary merit. John has been married for nineteen years to his wife, Cindy, and has two daughters, Kari and Lara. He is the founder and president of Encouraging Words, a ministry to families, based in Phoenix, Arizona.

Tom Whiteman is the founder and president of Life Counseling Services, a Christian counseling center in the Philadelphia area with ten locations and over thirty therapists. Dr. Whiteman is also an adjunct professor at Eastern College and the author or coauthor of ten books, including *The Complete Stress Management Workbook, The Fresh Start Divorce Recovery Workbook*, and *The Marriage Mender*. Tom is married to Lori and has three children, Elizabeth, Michelle, and Kurt.

H. Norman Wright is a licensed marriage, family, and child therapist who has pioneered premarital counseling programs throughout the country. Dr. Wright has taught graduate school for more than thirty years and is the founder of Christian Marriage Enrichment, in Tustin, California. He is in demand as a conference and seminar speaker and is the author of more than sixty books, including *Communication: Key to Your Marriage; The Seasons of a Marriage; Always Daddy's Girl; Recovering from the Losses of Life;* and the best-selling *Quiet Times for Couples*. Norm has been married to his wife, Joyce, for more than thirty-five years.